ARCHAEOLOGICAL SURVEY OF INDIA.

NEW IMPERIAL SERIES, VOLUME XXI.

CHALUKYAN ARCHITECTURE

INCLUDING EXAMPLES FROM THE BALLARI DISTRICT, MADRAS PRESIDENCY.

ARCHAEOLOGICAL SURVEY OF INDIA.

NEW IMPERIAL SERIES, VOLUME XXI.

CHALUKYAN ARCHITECTURE

INCLUDING EXAMPLES FROM THE BALLARI DISTRICT, MADRAS PRESIDENCY.

BY

ALEXR. REA, M.R.A.S.,

SUPERINTENDENT, ARCHAEOLOGICAL SURVEY,
MADRAS.

GYAN

Published by

Gyan Publishing House
5, Ansari Road
Daryaganj, New Delhi-110002
Phone: 011-47034999, 9811692060
E-mail: books@gyanbooks.com

Distribution Network
gyanbooks.com
India, USA, Canada, UK, Australia, France

ISBN : 978-81-212-2654-7 (HB)
First Published, 1896

2nd Impression 2021

Printed at: Gyan Press, Delhi.

Chalukyan Architecture
Author: Alexr. Rea

ARCHÆOLOGICAL SURVEY OF INDIA.

NEW IMPERIAL SERIES, VOLUME XXI.

CHÂLUKYAN ARCHITECTURE;

INCLUDING EXAMPLES FROM THE BALLÂRI DISTRICT, MADRAS PRESIDENCY.

BY

ALEXR. REA, M.R.A.S.,

SUPERINTENDENT, ARCHÆOLOGICAL SURVEY, MADRAS.

MADRAS:

PRINTED AND PUBLISHED BY THE SUPERINTENDENT, GOVERNMENT PRESS.

CALCUTTA—Thacker, Spink & Co. BOMBAY—Thacker & Co., Ld.

LONDON—Trubner & Co. and W. H. Allen & Co.

LEIPZIG—Otto Harrassowitz.

1896.

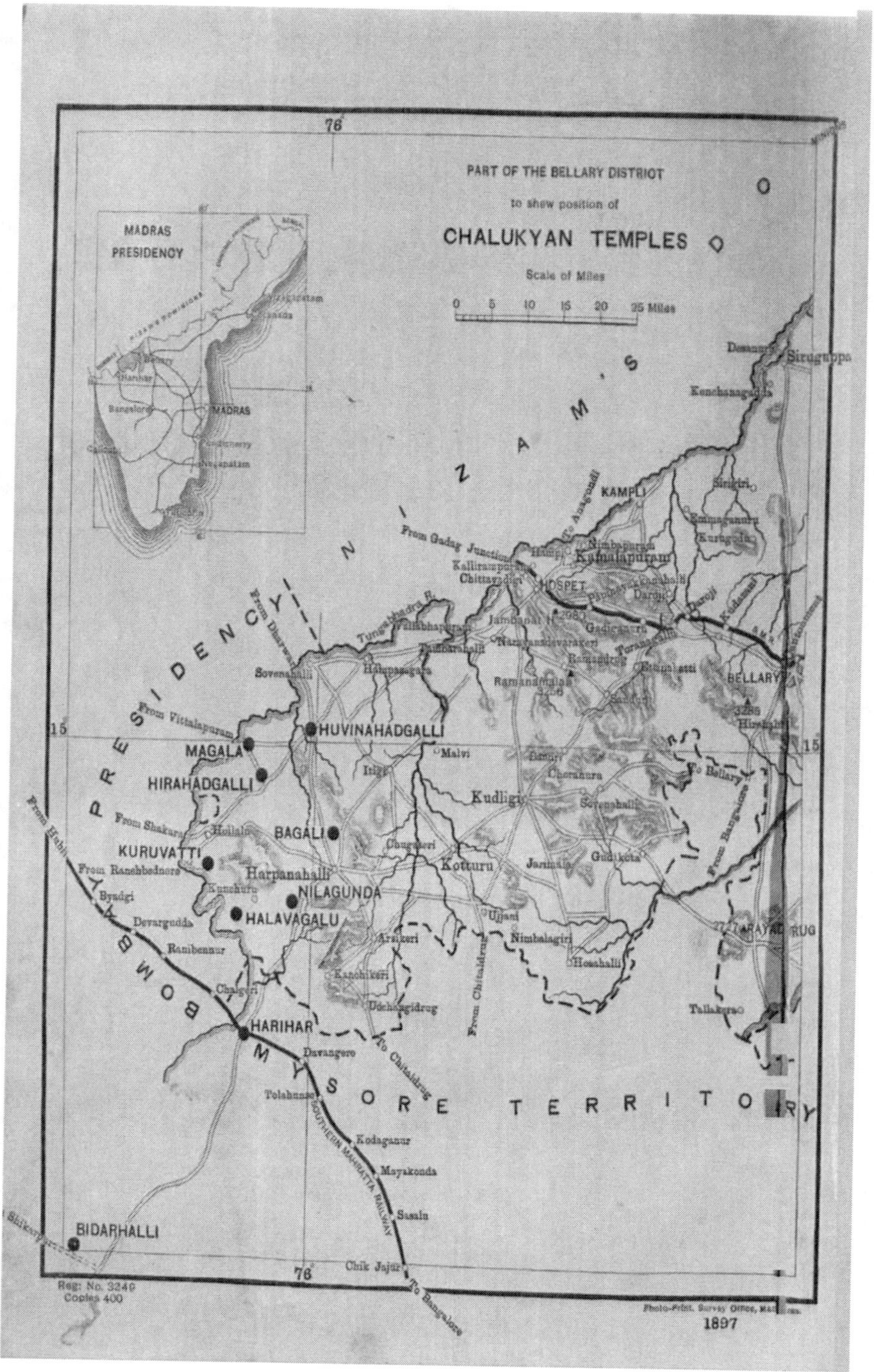
PART OF THE BELLARY DISTRICT
to shew position of
CHALUKYAN TEMPLES
Scale of Miles
0 5 10 15 20 25 Miles
MADRAS PRESIDENCY
MADRAS
Bellary
Harihar
Bangalore
NIZAM'S DOMINIONS
BOMBAY PRESIDENCY
MYSORE TERRITORY
76°
15
KAMPLI
Kamalapuram
HOSPET
BELLARY
HUVINAHADGALLI
MAGALA
HIRAHADGALLI
BAGALI
KURUVATTI
Harpanahalli
NILAGUNDA
HALAVAGALU
Kudligi
Kotturu
HARIHAR
Davangere
Siruguppa
BIDARHALLI
SOUTHERN MAHRATTA RAILWAY
To Bangalore
To Chitaldrug
From Hubli
Ranibennur
Chik Jajur
Reg: No. 3249
Copies 400
Photo-Print, Survey Office, Madras.
1897

CONTENTS.

LIST OF PLATES.

ERRATUM

TO

"CHÂLUKYAN ARCHITECTURE."

(*ARCHÆOLOGICAL SURVEY OF INDIA, NEW IMPERIAL SERIES, VOL. XXI.*)

In the title of plate CII *for* "Huvinahadgalli, Kesavasvami Temple" *read* "Halavagalu Kallesvara Temple."

great space of time can separate any of them; their details when minutely examined are similar in parts, though may be in individual instances, differently applied. The variations in the application or arrangement of parts in a design may be ascribed, not to the results of a widely separate period of the art, but to originality on the part of the workman. In this style, as in others Indian, the main arrangement of certain parts is fixed by rule; but great latitude is allowed to the workman who carries out the design. In this, lies the great beauty of these temples, and of every several part composing them. A broad unvarying principle can be traced in every example, however varied the design may be, a principle in no way effaced by the individuality observable in its overlying details. Many considerations doubtless had their share in the fixing of the class of plan adopted, the greatness of the god to whom the temple was to be erected, the sanctity of the site, or the number of shrines required for lesser or attendant deities.

There are three well defined forms of plan represented. One is a plurality of similar shrines attached and opening on to an enclosed maṇḍapa and necessarily facing in different directions, but with the principal shrine opening towards the east. Another has a single shrine only, in the main building, with an enclosed maṇḍapa on its east. The third is an advance on the preceding, in that it has an open colonnade in front of the enclosed maṇḍapa.

The plan with three connected shrines is undoubtedly borrowed directly from the Jainas, and is one of the results of Jaina influence observable, though the buildings themselves are clearly Hindu. This is probably due to the Châlukyas having originally been adherents of the Jaina faith. The arrangement, as here carried out, rarely occurs in Hindu temples of later date. A modification of the feature is seen in some of the temples, in which only one main shrine is adopted, but in which it is still necessary to make provision for these minor deities. In these cases, side niches in the shrine are considered sufficient. Again, in a three-celled temple, with a lighted central hall, as at Mâgalâ, the three shrines have an equal amount of light. In the transition to a single shrine, placed at the dark end of a badly lighted maṇḍapa, the shrine was placed in almost total darkness. Latterly this came to be considered an advantage, or, at least, nothing was done to obviate it. At the transition, however, such an attempt was made, by the use of side lights, as we see at Huvinahaḍgalli and Kuruvatti. Some of the three-shrined temples have, in addition, a fourth cell detached from the main building, and facing the principal shrine. Such a subsidiary shrine, intended for a Basava, or other attendant on the principal god, is not unusual in other classes of temples, although in them it is usually given lesser prominence.

A matter to be observed in the plans of the shrines is, that their main exterior lines are rectangular, and not star-shaped, as are the principal of those in this style described by Mr. Fergusson.[1]

The form of the plan is important, for its outline is carried up and repeated in the storeys of the tower, giving to it its own particular character. A star-shaped plan is ill-adapted to, and does not, so far as I am aware, ever appear in a storeyed tower built on the lines of those of the Dravidians. Only three of the buildings, Hîrahaḍagalli, Kuruvatti and Nîlaguṇḍa, retain their towers in original outline. The last would certainly have three, and probably four; but has now only one. The others have it only in part, or entirely away. In the latter case, however, we have no difficulty in assuming what the form has been, for it is repeated again and again in miniature over the niches of the walls. That these representations were true copies of the original, as far as could be on such a small scale, is seen by

[1] *Ibid.*, p. 44.

comparison, where the tower yet remains. Thus at Mâgalâ no trace of the three shrine towers exists; but the form of outline is preserved on the wall niches. A peculiarity is noticed both at the building mentioned, and at Hîrahaḍagalli. Some of the lesser of these miniature towers, or those placed, not over the main niche, but on pilasters or other projections on the walls, have a curved northern outline. This must be ascribed to the effects of the more typical Jaina style from which this was derived, and where such a tower was actually used in construction over a star-shaped plan. The carvers evidently had in idea such a design before them, but on a Dravidianized plan could only use it as a decorative and not as a constructive feature. The varied designs of the numerous wall niches are strikingly noticeable. Most of the niches are now vacant, but from the characters of their architectural details, the class of image which occupied any particular one can be ascertained. Mr. Fergusson has pointed out [1] that "the great gods—such as Brahmâ, Vishṇu, Śiva and Indra—have umbrella canopies. The incarnations of Vishṇu, their saktis or wives, and minor deities have symmetrical canopies springing from both sides and forming something like a regular arch. Apsaras or heavenly maidens, mortals, and the lowest class of gods have unsymmetrical canopies springing from one side only." Examples of all these classes occur, with the addition of the architectural canopy, in combination with the floral one in the more ornate buildings. In those less ornate, the architectural canopy alone is employed.

The Dravidian form of the towers has been pointed out. Not only in the towers, but in the treatment of their whole external outline, the temples exhibit a preponderence of Dravidian forms. They might best be described as an embodiment of Châlukyan details engrafted on a Dravidian building. This is probably partly due to their outlying position, and the resulting effects of adjoining styles of architecture, of a different class, practised outside the sphere of Châlukyan influence.

No one who has examined any single specimen of Châlukyan carving can have failed to note its marvellous intricacy and artistic finish in even the minutest details. The workman was no doubt greatly assisted by the pliability of the material in which he had to work; but his complete mastery of the art is none the less remarkable. On the temple of Guduk, Colonel Meadows Taylor makes some remarks which have quite as appropriate an application here. He states [2] "It is impossible to describe the exquisite finish of the pillars of the interior of this temple, which are of black hornblende, or greenstone, nor to estimate how they were completed in their present condition without they were turned in a lathe, yet there can be little doubt that these pillars, which support the roof and body of the temple, were in fact set up originally as rough masses of rock, and afterwards carved into their present forms." The latter statement is true as regards the carving, not only on the piers, but elsewhere. There seems, however, abundant evidence to show that the piers were not set up in a rough unmoulded form, but actually turned in a primitive though effective kind of lathe. Of the carving he writes, "the carving on some of the pillars and of the lintels and architraves of the doors is quite beyond description. No chased work in gold or silver could possibly be finer, and the patterns to this day, are copied by goldsmiths, who take casts and moulds from them, but fail in representing the sharpness and finish of the original. By what tools this very hard, tough stone could have been wrought and polished as it is, is not at all intelligible at the present day; nor indeed from whence the large blocks of greenstone were brought; and in popular estimation nothing short of the miraculous creation of these temples, of which there are many legends, suffices to account for them."

---

[1] *Ibid.*, p. 5[illegible].

[2] *Ibid.*, pp. 47, 48.

The ornament is generally completely undercut, and sometimes attached to the solid masonry by the most slender of stalks. It has often the effect of an incrustation of foliage placed on the wall. Its general principle seems to have been based on a broad mass of foliage standing in high relief from a narrow but deeply cut background.

The toning effects of age, which, leaving the details as sharp as when they left the sculptor's hands, have imbued them with their varying shades of brown, and given them added beauty.

Châlukyan carving forms the veriest contrast to the earliest works of this species of Indian art—the Buddhist. Each has its own particular beauties, but the one may be described as an embodiment of conventional forms, for natural treatment is seldom if ever adopted. The other consists largely of natural foliage. The latter may be described as a more refined form of art in that the effect is attained, not by a high contrast of light and shade, but by the very delicacy of the bas-relief in which it is cut. Châlukyan sculpture on the other hand—whether in the intricate geometrical patterns of the ceilings, or the foliated work which covers every part of the buildings—exhibits the greatest possible exuberance of varied forms, boldly designed and finely executed to the minutest detail. Its effect is greatly enhanced by the deeply cut background. This, combined with the fineness of the detail, makes it equally effective, whether viewed closely or at a distance.

Except in a few of the lesser structures at Bâgali, all the temples are constructed of a species of black hornblende, as porous as marble, and with much of its effects. It is said to be soft on being quarried, and to harden on exposure to the weather. It is thus admirably adapted to sculptural work; for, while it readily lends itself to the carver's skill, centuries of exposure do not diminish its sharpness.

Carved blocks were first dressed to the required outline, fixed in their positions in the building and then carved *in situ*.

The circular columns have generally a profusion of delicate string-like mouldings, all perfectly worked, and often bearing marks showing that they were actually turned. The process seems to have been to select a block of stone, rough-dress it to the requisite height and diameter, fix it upright, attached to beams in a pit, revolve the stone on its axis by bullock power, and apply tools to the revolving surface till the desired outline was attained.

As to the quality of the tools or chisels used by the workmen who executed these carvings, we have no means of information; nor are we likely to have any, beyond the self-evident fact that they were perfectly suited to their purpose. With a deeply cut but extremely narrow background to the foliage, often with the merest eyehole into which the chisel could be inserted, the carving tools must have been of the very slenderest make. A high quality of steel has been in use in India from the earliest times, so no difficulty would be experienced in their production. Were the subjects of ancient Indian art on a parallel with those of the Egyptians, we might learn their form from their carvings, but the sculptors seem to have been more concerned with the representation of the arms of their warriors and the ornaments of their gods than the sculpturing of homely implements or the tools of handicraftsmen.

CHAPTER II.

BÂGALI.

KALLÊŚVARA TEMPLE.

The village stands 8 miles east by north of the taluk head-quarters of Harpanahaḷḷi.

The temple is, as regards arrangement of plan, one of the most complete of the group included in this volume. Excepting Harihar, it presents a design essentially different to any of them (Pl. I.). It consists of a main shrine and enclosed maṇḍapa opening on to an open-pillared mahâmaṇḍapa of cruciform plan. Other detached shrines stand in positions around. The shrine and enclosed front maṇḍapa are, in detail, mainly Dravidian, with Châlukyan features interspersed. Thus, the doors of this central maṇḍapa are in the latter style; the great open colonnade is wholly so. This arrangement of the mahâmaṇḍapa appears at Harihar in Maisûr, and in many of those illustrated by Mr. Fergusson in his work on this style of architecture.[1]

In the main west shrine is a liṅga, of only a few inches diameter and height, placed on a pedestal. Against the north wall is a small stone bench supported on posts for placing images or vessels used in worship. The door is plainly moulded.

The door-way to the ante-chamber is a well sculptured one. It has dvârapâlakas on each side; and a sculptured panel on the lintels, with figures of Gaja Lakshmi, Brahmâ, Îśvara and Vishṇu.

In the front enclosed maṇḍapa are four massive piers in square and polygonal sections, with wide capitals and brackets. Responding pilasters are on the walls. One corner of the maṇḍapa has been partitioned off to form a shrine. On the ceiling is a lotus leaf patera. The east and south doorways are well carved, but the detail of the latter is overlaid with thick coats of whitewash.

The design and arrangement of the piers of the open mahâmaṇḍapa will be seen on a reference to the plan, elevation and section (Pls. I, II, fig. 2, and III, fig. 4). A moulded stylobate, with bench inside, surrounds the whole. No two piers are exactly alike, though in corresponding pairs a general outline is observed. The plans are elaborately cut in simple or intersecting squares, circular, star-shaped, octagonal, and various other polygonal forms. These are varied by squares with the angles checked, and polygons with convex, concave or acute angular sides. The one form is usually carried up through every moulding from base to capital. The four central piers are, as usual, more ornate, and stand on sculptured pedestals.

A number of images have been set up at various places in the building. A Nandi stands incentre facing the shrine.

Several of the compartments of the ceiling are carved in circular and diagonal panels; the most noteworthy is that in the central compartment. Their general outline is shown in

---

[1] *Architecture in Dharwar and Mysore.*

the different compartments on plate I. The diagonal ceilings are usually flat, while those circular are dome-shaped.

The base of the building is buried under the accumulation of soil formed during the centuries that have elapsed since the temple was erected. A pit was dug at one point, where the outline of the mouldings can be seen. The base mouldings are uncarved, as are also the blocks on the parapet which surmounts the deeply carved cornice.

The walls of the shrine and attached maṇḍapa have plain pilasters and Dravidian details. The shrine tower is modern brick-and-plaster work laid over the ruined ancient masonry.

At the north end of the colonnade, and opening into it, is a shrine of Narasiṁhasvâmi with a fine sculptured image of the god. The base of the shrine is moulded, and is the only ancient portion of the building. The superstructure is modern. The more intricate form of the original building is preserved in the outline of the base.

To the east of the mahâmaṇḍapa is a small shrine of Sûrya Narâyanasvâmi, with two images inside. The walls are in the same style, and designed similarly to the main west shrine. Close to it is a well.

At the north-west of the courtyard are four other shrines. One, dedicated to the Vishṇappa liṅga, is built in granite. Another of the Virubakshi liṅga has a black-stone shrine, as in the main one, and a maṇḍapa with square piers. Around it stand ten inscribed stones. Other two shrines containing the Râma liṅga, and an image of Sîtêśvara, are of common stone and plain workmanship. These buildings, if not actually contemporaneous with the main shrine, are probably only a few years later. They have been ruined in parts and patched up with masonry or mud.

On the south of the court, and hidden by the lofty bund of a neighbouring reservoir, are three maṇḍapas. In a line with them stand twenty inscribed stones. One of these maṇḍapas has in connection, a shrine of Vîrabhadra. They have plain stone walls and piers. The sloping construction of the roof of one of them is elsewhere illustrated.

There are a few other temples of lesser note in the village.

The Chânna Basava temple is illustrated on plate III, figs. 1, 2 and 3. It is a small building constructed of freestone. Owing to the mode of roofing, with large sloping slabs projecting at the eaves—which meet and necessarily require support at or near the centre—two pillars appear in the shrine. A similar mode of roofing is seen in the porches of the Kêsavasvâmi temple at Huvinahaḍgalli; and again, in a form less defined, in the Kallêśvara temple at that place. The portion of the floor, on which stand the bull and liṅga, is slightly raised above the front of the room. The door to the shrine enclosure is well sculptured in blackstone in the same style as that of the ante-chamber in the Kallêśvara temple. The exterior piers in the open front maṇḍapa are square and octagon in plan, and are cut at the necking to carry the brackets which support the beam under the roofing slabs. The four central piers are of similar massive form, and, on account of the increased height necessary to carry the beams to the top of the slope of the slabs, have capitals under the brackets. A plain stylobate surrounds the maṇḍapa.

The Hitadêvaru temple is a small ruined Châlukyan building in blackstone. It comprises a shrine and front maṇḍapa. The chief feature of note is a doorway sculptured similarly to that above referred to.

The Sangan Basappa temple is another black stone temple of small size, with features of no particular note, except a well sculptured image of Kallêśvara.

The village contains a few other shrines of different style and more modern date.

Plate IV.

Nine piers from the mahâmaṇḍapa.

In this portion of the temple there are in all fifty-nine detached piers. Almost every one differs from another, if not in general design, at least in some or other of the details. Even where the plan or outline resembles another, they are so arranged as to give not only the appearance of great diversity of form, but a perfect artistic harmony throughout. Their arrangement can be studied from plates I and III, fig. 4.

It will be seen that one style of contour is adopted in almost all the examples, but the skilful introduction of ornaments and small mouldings, or a slight alteration in their proportions, is sufficient to give each an original character of its own. Each stands on a moulded base. The lower portion of the column is upright, and either plain, moulded, or ornamented. A cluster of minute ornaments divides this from the bulging middle portion of the pier. The shaft then tapers by a succession of mouldings into the necking; and another series of mouldings, of which the most prominent is one not unlike the classical torus with a fillet on its face, connects it with the upper portion of the capital and abacus. This is the general form observed in almost all Châlukyan piers. But a study of these examples will show what diversity can be obtained in what is practically one design. The greatest variety is, however, attained by the form of the plan. Sometimes this is continued right up from base to capital. In others, the different forms of square, circle, octagon and polygon are embodied in the one pier. The latter section is variously employed; thus we find concave and convex flutes, stars, squares with various curves or notches on the angles, and many others. Fig. 1 has a plan with small shafts running up from base to capital. The general plan of fig. 2 is circular, with the lower portion square and ornamented with niches. Fig. 3 has hollow flutes and a square base. Fig. 4 is star-shaped, formed by two intersecting squares. Fig. 5 has the lower part composed of two squares separated by an octagon, and circular capital. Fig. 6 is in general plan square throughout, with a right-angled triangle notched in at each corner. The plan of fig. 7 is a variety of that of fig. 6; the notching or chamfer on the angles is convex. Fig. 8 is a twelve-pointed star. Fig. 9 is an elaborated form of fig. 4; the faces on the two intersecting squares are moulded with small stepped fillets.

Plate V.

Fig. 1.—The east doorway to the ardha-maṇḍapa. This is a good example of a Châlukyan doorway. Though it has the usual features common to its class, the variety of treatment of the detail gives it an individuality of its own. Features which may be specially noted in comparison with other examples are the row of small seated images over the cornice, the drops under, and the lions on the brackets over the piers.

Fig. 2.—The door to the antarâla maṇḍapa. Perforated stone windows occupy the place of the usual broad and varied succession of jamb mouldings, found in doors occupying other positions. This introduction of a window is necessary to give an increase of light to what would otherwise be a very dark interior. Variety of detail may be noted on the small floral arches supported on brackets over the cornice, the panels on the middle of the piers, and the figure panels over Gajalakshmi between the cornice and the door lintel. The latter are necessary as a central feature or stop to the perforated windows which return over the door. For comparison, another example at Huvinahaḍgalli, where the window is carried across the top without a break, may be noted. (Pl. XCV.)

Plate VI.

Fig. 1.—An enlarged drawing of the exterior south-west corner of the shrine, showing the base, wall with pilasters and niches, and he cornice over. Its Dravidian characteristics will be apparent. The mouldings of the base, for example, have nothing of the clear cut sharpness of the other style. On the other hand, the carved blocks on the cornice have a slight touch of the Châlukyan element.

Fig. 2.—Two of a series of small figures on the north wall.

Fig. 3.—A sketch of the madapalli or cooking room. It forms one of the three maṇḍapas which are partly covered by the bund of the tank which adjoins the south side of the temple.

Plate VII.

Figs. 1 to 6.—Images in the mahâmaṇḍapa.

Fig. 1.—Dêvêndra or Indra standing on a moulded pedestal, with a canopy resting on piers behind. Two females stand at his feet. His vehicle, Airâvata, is in a panel in front of the base.

Fig. 2.—A seated figure of Śarasvati on a moulded base with carved canopy behind.

Fig. 3.—A portion of a carved slab, the principal figure of which is Brahmâ. He is seated under a canopy with makaras on his right and left. From the mouths of these beasts spring the scrolls of the canopy. The animals on his left are supported on a pilaster; and on their backs rests a small shrine with a figure inside. Overhead are shown some of the principal deities, riding on their vehicles. Below are other figures. The portion of the slab broken away, would contain similar groups with Îśvara and Vishṇu as the principal figures.

Fig. 4.—Durga and the buffalo-headed Mahishâsura. With a sword in one of her right hands she slays the Asura. She tramples one of the Rakshasas under foot, and at the same time taps him on the head with her club. The various arms hold different weapons. In one of the left is the bow, while one of her right hands draws an arrow from the quiver on her back.

Fig. 5.—Anantaśâyana reclining on his serpent couch, guarded by the hoods of the nâga. His wife Lakshmi keeps watch at the head of the couch. His weapons are ranged in front.

Fig. 6.—A large image of the Vishṇu avatâr of Narasiṁha slaying the tyrannical monarch Hirânyakasipu. The king's devout son Prahlâda and others stand below.

Plate VIII.

Figs. 1 and 2 in this plate represent the plan and section of the principal ceiling in the mahâmaṇḍapa. It is built in rings of courses, tapering to the summit, in the form of a cupola. A very deep dropstone (fig. 3) is let down through the crown. It is carved with deities on each face, and animals below. The different rings are angular, with a series of cusps cut on the angles. At the eight cardinal points on the lowest course are projecting blocks, carved with the Ashtadikpâlakas. These are illustrated on plate II, fig. 1. Four of them have figure-sculptured panels above them. The under sides of the blocks are carved with pateras and other ornament.

CHAPTER III.

MÂGALÂ.

Veṇugopâlasvâmi Temple.

A village standing 10 miles west of Huvinahaḍgalli.

The plan of the temple is composed of a spacious central hall, with an entrance on the south side, and a shrine entering off each of the three others. (Plate IX.) These three shrines would originally be occupied by the Trimûrti or Hindu triad, Brahmâ, Śiva and Vishṇu. The former would be in the usual place in the centre, with Vishṇu on his right and Śiva on his left. The temple was a Vaishnava one, and, while still retaining the relative positions of the gods, it was necessary in the interests of sectarian belief, which considered its own particular god the most important, that it should be placed in the usual position facing the east. This was attained by fixing the temple in the unusual position of having its principal façade to the south.

In the centre of the porch is the entrance door, with comparatively simple moulded architraves. The porch walls are thin, and constructed of mullions and transoms crossing each other so as to form three vertical rows of small square openings. The cross bars are carved in floral designs. On a raised stone bench inside the south wall of the porch, stand four delicately carved circular columns. Other six piers stand on the floor of the hall. Four of these form the usual central group raised on a square pedestal; they have boldly carved capitals and figure brackets. Against the inner west wall of the porch, is a small niche, with a moulding under, and a cornice over. Inside it, standing on the floor against the wall, is a panel with a row of nine-seated figures, each with a canopy overhead. Pilasters are placed against the walls of the hall, responding to the six central piers.

The three doors entering off the main hall are exquisite pieces of design and workmanship, that on the west being the finest. Those on the north and east have small moulded pilasters on each side, with a vertical row of small square perforated openings through the wall. Each perforation is fitted with a diamond shaped ornament. Along the top of each door is a cornice, ornamented with miniature towers.

The west door is similar in design to the others, but more richly carved. In place of the side perforations, there are upright rows of small figures seated inside a series of circular ornaments. In the other two temples of Hîrahaḍagalli and Nîlaguṇḍa, which have, or had three main shrines, the principal one is on the west, with its door facing the east and entrance door. The two subsidiary shrines form wings on each side of it. The west shrine at Mâgalâ does not face the outer entrance door as in the others; yet that it has been the chief one is shown by the superior richness of its entrance.

There is a moulded niche in each of the side interior wall-spaces of the hall; the north wall is blank. At the north-east corner stands an inscribed stone, with an elaborately worked representation of a liṅga, bull, and emblems on the top.

Each of the three shrines enters through a square ante-chamber. The doors directly entering the shrines are finely carved, though less richly than those opening on the hall. In the east shrine is a well-carved figure on a pedestal, with a canopy over; a Nandi is in the chamber in front of it.

One of the glories of this temple consists in its ceilings, which are of very varied and beautiful design. Every compartment comprised in the building is thus decorated. Their initial construction is the usual arrangement of flat and circular overlapping slabs. The finest are those in the hall, the one in the central compartment being particularly elaborate and lofty. The building is shown in section on plates X and XI.

On the exterior of the building, a moulded base, with an upper row of lions, vyâlis and other figures, surrounds the temple. (Plates XII and XIII.)

The wall pilasters are narrow, and are plain up to the mid height of the walls. The upper half is hidden in a profusion of foliage and candelabras. The latter feature occurs at Hirahadagalli; but there they are turned on to the walls. Here the wall-spaces are otherwise occupied. They support canopies and miniature towers which occupy the upper portions. On each of the three external faces of the shrines is a deeply recessed niche. Surmounting the wall heads is an ornamental cornice, narrow when compared with the deep overhanging cornice of the porch. Above are rows of elaborately carved blocks and sculptured panels of varied design. Each shrine has undoubtedly had a tower; but the exterior work is now away, and only masses of rough blocks remain on the roof.

No worship is conducted at the building. It is known as the 'Jaina temple.'

Plate XIV.

One of the projecting bays of the north wall. The work being in a finely grained blackstone, remains as sharply cut as when it left the hands of the sculptor. The central object is, as usual, a niche surmounted by a miniature representation of a shrine tower; the front of its main cornice is broken away, but its detail and ornament can be ascertained from that remaining over the side pilasters. Underneath is an ornamental sômasûtra for carrying off the water from the shrine inside. The principal feature in the base is a row of lions along the upper member. They are shown in the act of rending birds, elephants and other animals. Above are a series of short pilasters, surmounted by small bell-shaped towers. Between them are long pilasters which extend up to the under side of the wall-head cornice. The upper portion of the wall is ornamented with vyâli's heads and projecting lamp brackets.

Plate XV.

Fig. 1.—An ornament on the base. It is one of a series on the upper member of the base. A figure of a deity—in this case Ganêsa—sits in a niche, flanked by rampant lions, and surmounted by a floral arch.

Fig. 2.—A floral arch over a niche on the south wall.

Fig. 3 is a monolithic figure of Anantaśâyana from a small temple at Holâlu.

Plate XVI.

One of the large pilasters on the north wall. The lower portion shows the main base of the building on which the pilaster rests. The plan of the pilaster from base to capital is rectangular, with stepped corners. The wall base projects opposite each of these pilasters; its mouldings also follow the plan of the pilaster.

Plate XVII.

The ceiling in the central compartment of the mahâmaṇḍapa. It is the principal and most highly ornate of the many fine ceilings in this temple; its position will be seen by a reference to the sectional drawings of the temple (Plates X and XI). The carved rectangular lintels, which rest on the four corner piers, support the upper circular portion. The carved blocks at the eight cardinal points, with representations of the Ashtadikpâlakas, rest immediately over the beams. The mouldings, from the under side of these blocks upwards are circular. Spandrels or triangular spaces are thus formed on the under side at the four corners. The carved work on these is shown on the plan. The work is built in large circular faced blocks, or courses of blackstone. The large and finely carved drop, or centre piece, is in a single block, let down from the top. The carving presents great variety of design, and its effect can be but faintly represented by any drawing.

Plate XVIII.

A ceiling in the east end of the porch. In this part of the building there are six compartments, each with a carved ceiling. The two in the outer corners are both of a design similar to the one under note. The ceiling—as are most of those in this temple—is profusely ornamented. The lower portion is square, the two intermediate intersecting octagons, and the crown, circular. The central drop is small. At the foot of the circular portion is a series of fans, each with a drop in its centre. The connecting space between these is flat, ornamented with leaves. The various triangular spaces formed by the junction of the circles, octagon, and square are filled with floral ornament.

Plates XIX and XX.

Two of the diagonal ceilings in the mahâmaṇḍapa. They are formed of richly ornamented flat slabs laid across the corners. In the centre is a circular cupola.

Plate XXI.

Figs. 1 and 2.—Ornaments on the cornices of niches in the mahâmaṇḍapa.

Fig. 3.—Carving on the top of an inscribed stone standing near the temple. It represents a Châlukyan temple with three shrines, each surmounted by a tower. In the centre shrine is a linga with a worshipper. A deity stands in each of the side shrines. On one outer side is a Nandi, and on the other a cow and calf. Overhead is a representation of the sun and moon.

Fig. 4.—On the entrance side of the mahâmaṇḍapa are a number of perforated stone windows. The figure shows the ornament with which the cross-bars and jambs are covered.

Plate XXII.

A finely carved blackstone image in the shrine.

Plate XXIII.

Fig. 1.—A carved sômasûtra at the side of the shrine. Its design is similar to another at Nîlagunda. (Plate LV.)

Fig. 2.—A wedge-shaped ornament on the front of the porch. From a vyâli's head springs some floral ornament; and a soldier armed with sword and shield stands in the ower coil.

Plate XXIV.

Fig. 1.—An ornamental block on the south side of the west shrine. A Vaishnava deity stands in the centre compartment, armed with various emblems, and holding a human head in one of his left hands. Beside him are two ascetics and a deer. Around the panel is some floral ornament. In each of the side wings is a female chauri bearer.

Fig. 2.—A panel situate close to that above described. The panel group represents the same subject as the other. On each side is a Châlukyan pier which has supported a floral canopy now broken away.

Plate XXV.

Fig. 1.—A pedimental panel over the cornice. It is a fine example, with details of ornament similar to others already described.

Fig. 2.—A detail of the front cornice, showing a group of carved panel blocks.

Fig. 3.—A horizontal band of ornament on the door to the north shrine.

Plate XXVI.

A niche on the side of the entrance porch. It is similar to the others, placed on the walls of the temple. Like the niches at Huvinahaḍgalli, a small figure stands inside. The niche cornice has sufficient projection to give it the appearance of a canopy. Over the miniature tower is a floral arch. Projecting lamp brackets spring from the upper portion of the main wall pilasters. This feature appears in a more ornate form at Hîrahaḍagalli.

Plate XXVII.

The lower part of the left architrave of a door in the mahâmaṇḍapa, showing the dvârapâlakas at the base, and details of the ornament. The lines of ornament inside the pilasters also return along the face of the lintel. The doorway from which this is taken is elsewhere illustrated.

Plate XXVIII.

The carving surmounting the parapet over the front doorway. This piece of carving forms a portion of a course which runs round the entire building. The carved corner blocks on each side of the centre slab, are similarly carved on two faces; they are placed over each of the corners formed by the numerous recesses and projections on the different façades.

Plate XXIX.

A panel built in the wall of the mahâmaṇḍapa, at the left side of the entrance. In it are the Navagṛînas, or nine celestials. Each is seated on a pedestal under a canopy. Vishṇu occupies the centre, as becomes a panel in a temple of that deity, with Îśvara and Ganêśa on his extreme right and left. When these three chief deities are thus brought in combination in temples of the opposite sect, the group is differently arranged.

Plate XXX.

Fig. 1.—One of the four central piers in the mahâmaṇḍapa. The base, and the abacus of the capital are square; the latter has a notch out of the four corners. The body of the shaft is circular, having been—as is the case with all these circular columns—turned and grooved with a chisel in a pit.

Fig. 2.—A sketch of the brackets supporting the beams over one of the four central piers in the mahâmaṇḍapa. There are four similar brackets over each of these piers. They have groups of musicians on the under side, with floral ornament and rolls over.

Fig. 3.—A continuous ornament on the front cornice.

Plate XXXI.

Figs. 1 and 2.—Ornamental bands on the body of the four central piers in the mahâmaṇḍapa. The mouldings—on which these ornaments are—are circular. The piers are shown on the section of the building.

CHAPTER IV.

HÎRAHAḌAGALLI.

KATTÊŚVARA TEMPLE.

The village stands nine miles south-west of the taluk head-quarters of Huvinahaḍgalli. It was here that I found the copper-plate grant of the Pallava king Śivaskandavarman, published by Professor G. Bühler, in Part I of the *Epigraphia Indica.*

The plan of the temple now comprises the principal shrine at the west end; an enclosed maṇḍapa in front, with a building at each side; and another detached shrine facing the main one, with an enclosed maṇḍapa in front of it. The plan as it now stands—disfigured with modern walls of mud and masonry—does not represent the original one in its entirety. (pl. XXXII.) Some foundations which stand in the open space between the separated buildings show, that the plan has been one resembling that at Bâgali (pl. I). The architectural details in this case, however, are purely Châlukyan. In the complete building, the present west shrine being the central one, probably had another on one or other of the sides of the enclosed maṇḍapa in the front, as at Harihar. Two shrines at present stand there, but the foundations only are of ancient construction. That on the north is mud built, while the one opposite forms a porch constructed of ancient materials enclosed by mud walls. The entrances to these side shrines may have been through enclosed passages as at Mâgalâ and Nilaguṇḍa, or through an open porch as at Harihar. The foundations appearing in front of the maṇḍapa would be those of a pillared mahâmaṇḍapa similar to but of lesser extent than those existing at Bâgali and Harihar. The present east shrine would be connected with the main building in the same manner as the corresponding shrine at Nilaguṇḍa. The pillars of the connecting vestibule still stand, but enclosed by modern walls. Of this subsidiary shrine, only the foundations and base are ancient, the walls built over them are of plain modern construction.

In the west shrine is the principal liṅga worshipped. The door is richly carved, and has a perforated window on each side. The ante-chamber in front is unusually narrow: in these other temples it more nearly approaches a square. In the front enclosed maṇḍapa are four finely carved piers in the centre, and a number of images in the corners. Mahishâsuramardini stands in the north-east corner; Pârvatisamêtha in the south-east; Sarasvati in the south-west; and in the other, Ganêśa and a slab, with nine seated figures, similar to one at Mâgalâ. In the side porches, converted by mud walls into shrines, are,—Nârâyanadêva on the north, and a liṅga on the south. On the raised platform in the centre of the maṇḍapa is placed a Nandi, facing the main shrine. The ceilings of these buildings are—with the exception of a patera in the centre of the front building—perfectly plain; and in decided contrast to the richness of the work on the exterior. The east entrance door to this building is elaborately carved. Somewhat to the front of it stand two inscribed stones; another stands on the east side of the south porch.

Around the main shrine and maṇḍapa, is a finely moulded and ornamented base, with carved blocks on the upper bands. In front of it, at the principal projections on the wall, are carved and perforated panels with a projecting niche and canopy over. By the side of the inches are slender pilasters, and the wall spaces between are filled in with miniature balconies, branched candelabras and other ornament. The general effect of the work in the building will be seen from the bay represented on plate XXXIII. No drawing, however, can adequately reproduce the rich and varied effect of the original with its beautiful design and workmanship, its light and shade, and varying tints of colour. A large proportion of the carving is perforated and only attached to the wall by a few stems. On this account, much of it has been broken away.

The tower over the western shrine, is almost complete to the śikara; some displacement of stones on one of the sides however, has been caused by plants. The design is formed of a pyramidal series of stories, each recessed behind the one below it. The same profusion of ornament observable on the walls is carried right up to the fine circular kalaśa on the summit.

Plate XXXIII.

A portion of the wall on the north side. Every detail of the carved work is as minutely finished as jewellery. Through age the stones have acquired a gloss and a rich chocolate colour which considerably heighten the artistic effect. The walls are spaced into a series of projecting bays, each divided into three parts; the central part projects in front of those on either side. The lower base is plainly moulded, without ornament. The upper base has also plain mouldings, but carved blocks with vyâli and makara heads are placed at every angle and return of the members.

In the bay represented on the plate, a sômasûtra, or spout for carrying off water from the shrine, projects over the base, and rests on an ornamental block with a carved panel on its front. The upper walls of the bay are divided into three parts by pilasters, the central one projecting beyond the others. On this central projection is a niche and a miniature balcony, with supporting lions underneath, and a carved moulding overhanging and acting as a canopy to the sômasûtra below. The niche has a cornice and tower, worked into the minutest detail, a perfect copy in miniature of the tower placed over the shrine roof. An image would at one time stand inside the niche. Smaller niches, with a figure carved inside, are on the spaces on each side. Below them are brackets projecting from the pilasters. The pilasters have foliated bases, and moulded capitals with ornamental neckings. From the necks spring ornamental curved lamp brackets.

Plate XXXIV.

Fig. 1.—A small projecting niche on the north side wall. The design is unique, in that it is a miniature representation of a shrine with base, parapet and entrance steps, columns, cornice, tower, and an image standing inside. It is supported on a bracket springing from a pilaster. The others on the walls are of similar design.

Fig. 2.—A ceiling slab found buried in the ground beside the ruined mahâmandapa. It evidently once formed the capping or centre piece of the principal ceiling in that building. The intertwining stems are for the most part, completely undercut. The figure is illustrated in the *Technical Art Series* 1891.

Fig. 3.—A carved panel on the front cornice, having an elephant fitted with the usual trappings.

Fig. 4.—A small carved block on the front cornice.

Plate XXXV.

This plate represents the east doorway of the temple. There are six tiers of carved mouldings and a pilaster on each side of the entrance, and each has a dvârapâlaka in a niche underneath. The inner line of the architrave has a row of diamond-shaped ornaments with flowers between. The second has tiers of double nâgas, above each other; the alternate groups have their tails intertwined: the return along the top has single figures. The third row from the door, has single and double figures placed inside scrolls. Outside this, is a polygonal-sided pilaster with horizontal moulded bands at intervals; the projecting cup-shaped moulding under the capital is a feature somewhat unusual. Beyond the pilaster are two lines of scrolls,—one carved with human figures and the other with lions—and a vertical stem with branching leaves. Beyond the members of the door is a broad pilaster of the usual type.

Plate XXXVI.

The doorway to the west shrine. On each side of the entrance, is a perforated stone window, with a flowered vase under, and a row of haṁsas over. The dvârapâlakas in this case—under the door jambs—are unusually small. A quaint bit of carving is seen in the group of monkeys by the side of the gods and pinnacles over the cornice.

Plate XXXVII.

Ornaments on the west door.

Fig. 1.—A small upper horizontal running scroll.

Fig. 2.—A portion of the perforated side-lights, showing the ornaments on the stone cross bars.

Plate XXXVIII.

Fig. 1.—A small ornament above one of the niches on the front façade. The central panel, round which the ornament is clustered, is, in this example, circular, with a lion in place of the more usual image of a deity.

Fig. 2.—A terminal semi-circular panel from the west side of the temple. The centre is a vyâli's head. Around the top is a wavy ornament springing from two makaras. On the top is a vyâli's head.

Fig. 3.—A circular scroll enclosing a haṁsa, on the west doorway.

Fig. 4.—A small rectangular panel with a scroll.

Plate XXXIX.

Fig. 1.—An image of Narâyaṇasvâmi in the north shrine. It is highly carved, and, with the exception of two broken forearms, in good preservation. At the top of the slab are some curious little figures; several are seated on pedestals. Some of these have a reference to the avatârs of Vishṇu.

Fig. 2.—A group of images standing in the mahâmaṇḍapa. They represent Śiva, his wife Pârvati, and two sons. The style of carving is similar to that above noted.

Fig. 3.—An ornamental band on a pilaster on the south side.

Fig. 4.—A drop ornament on the front of the cornice.

Fig. 5.—A band similar to fig. 3.

Plate XL.

IMAGES STANDING IN THE MAHÂMAṆḌAPA.

Fig. 1.—A figure of Mahishâsuramardini. She is eight-armed, with a quiver on her back and various weapons in her hands. One of the left arms is broken. Below are a buffalo, a figure under her right foot, and a figure and lion fighting.

Fig. 2.—A seated figure of Sarasvati, with piers behind, supporting a scroll work canopy. One of her right arms is broken at the elbow. Underneath her seat is an inscription; her vehicle is carved on the front of the pedestal.

Fig. 3.—Narâyaṇadêva standing in front of an arched canopy. Various figures are seated overhead. A female stands on the front of each of the piers. Below, in front of the pedestal, is a row of seven curious figures with the bodies of men and the heads of beasts.

Plate XLI.

Fig. 1.—Ornament on the tower cornice.

Fig. 2.—An ornament on the back cornice.

Fig. 3.—Vyâli head and ornament over a niche on the back wall.

Plate XLII.

Fig. 1.—A carved ornament over the south cornice.

Fig. 2.—A drop ornament on the base of the south porch.

Fig. 3.—A balcony, in the form of a small shrine, in a niche on the south side. Its design is similar to another elsewhere described in detail. (Pl. XXXIV, fig. 1.)

Plate XLIII.

Fig. 1.—A carved panel block ornament on the tower cornice.

Fig. 2.—One of the balconies on the walls.

Plate XLIV.

Fig. 1.—One of the carved blocks surmounting a cornice on the back of the tower.

Fig. 2.—The carved pediment of a niche on the back wall.

Plate XLV.

Two carved blocks on the tower. The design is the usual one, with a small panel or niche enclosing one or more deities, surmounted by some floral work springing from a vyâli's head.

Plate XLVI.

Fig. 1.—A panel over the south doorway. In the centre, Śiva is seated on a lotus, with a canopy overhead, and a floral ornament on each side.

Fig. 2.—A smaller panel, with a figure of Brahmâ.

Fig. 3.—Ornaments on the capitals of the pilasters on the exterior of the north wall. These headings might almost be described as double capitals, one over the other, though the under is really only an extra deep and highly ornate necking. From each necking springs a bracket or candelabra attached to the wall between each pilaster. Under each bracket is a vyâli's head with floral stems springing from the mouth. The capitals above, are moulded without ornament.

Fig. 4.—A nâga stone in the east shrine. The ornament from which the tail rises, is Châlukyan in character.

Plate XLVII.

Figs. 1 and 2 are piers in the south porch and the maṇḍapa of the east shrine. The general design and outline of both are similar. The former occupies the more important position, and thus is more highly ornate than the other. The carved blocks at the body of the pier may be noted. The small pieces of fretwork on the capital, have so slender an attachment, that many have been broken away.

CHAPTER V.

NÎLAGUṆḌA.

Bhîmêśvara Temple.

A village in the Harpanahaḷḷi taluk, standing 6 miles west-south-west of the town of that name.

The plan of the temple consists of an enclosed hall with an entrance door on the east, and a shrine entering off each of the other sides. The east entrance is through a porch which connects the main building with a fourth shrine standing to the east in front of it. (Plate XLVIII.)

The east entrance door of the central hall is plain when compared with other examples of this feature. Inside the hall, four circular piers stand in the centre, and two other fluted circular shafts are attached to the corners of the ante-chambers of the two side shrines. These two chambers want the usual doorway connecting them with the central hall. The rooms themselves are, on plan, less than a square. With the main west shrine, the usual arrangement of having a door to the ante-chamber is adhered to, and the form of the plan approaches a square. At the two west corners of the hall are four figure niches in the walls. A Nandi stands facing the entrance to the west shrine. A liṅga is placed inside. In the other shrines stand vacant pedestals. In all these cells there is a small moulded table projecting from each side wall. These are said to have been for the placing of small metal images, or pûja utensils. The shrine doors are plainly moulded with pilasters and unornamented mouldings. The entrance screen of the west ante-chamber has some richly carved work.

The central ceiling of the hall is the only one on which a profusion of carving has been wrought; it resembles one excavated at Hîrahaḍagalli. The others, whose positions are shown on the plan, have plain slabs of the usual square, diagonal, and circular pattern.

The piers of the east porch are of massive form, with square and polygonal sides. The east shrine is almost a replicate of those on the wings.

The interior of the building is shown on plate XLIX.

The base around the exterior is of the usual design, with some of the blocks uncarved.

The pilasters on the walls are slender, and reach to the main cornice. Interspersed are a few, having the more massive proportions of detached piers, as also occurs at Kuruvatti.

Between, are lesser ones with the usual surmounting canopies and towers.

Around the west shrine only, are recessed niches. In these are mutilated figures of Kâlabhairava, Îśvara and Narasiṁha.

The tower over the west shrine is nearly complete, but the masonry is in parts much displaced by vegetation. Stones have fallen, and lie around the base. It is built in recessed storeys with pilasters, cornices and carved blocks. No traces of the other towers remain; and the rest of the building above the cornice is a ruin. (Plate L.)

Plate LI.

Fig. 1.—A corner pier in the mahâmaṇḍapa.

The contour of the mouldings is that usually found in Châlukyan piers. The plan is a sixteen-pointed star—in the complete circle—with a double plane on each of the surfaces.

These lines run up from base to capital, and the resulting multiplicity of vertical lines adds greatly to the general effect.

Fig. 2.—Ornamental details on the base of the shrine. These are small panels carved with figures and rampant lions on the different projections of the structure. At each angle of the ingoing face are corbels carved with makara heads.

Fig. 3.—A terminal ornament or pedimental block on the tower. The exterior is stepped over a floral scroll, which springs from makaras, and terminates in a vyâli's head. Inside is a figure of Subrahmaṇya, with two female fan bearers.

Fig. 4.—An ornament of similar class to fig. 3; but of different design. Each side is flanked by a rampant lion, with one of his forepaws resting on the uplifted hand of a person who kneels below. The interior panel is filled with scroll work.

Plate LII.

Fig. 1.—Dvârapâlakas at the door of the principal shrine.

Fig. 2.—A finely carved group of Dvârapâlakas. They stand on a moulded pedestal, under a canopy of carved scroll work. The group comprises three females, each being profusely ornamented with jewels, and bearing chauries and various emblems.

Figs. 3 and 4.—A fine blackstone central ceiling. On the four sides of the capitals of the supporting piers are moulded consoles. On the centre of the soffit of the four enclosing beams is a floral carved patera, which is repeated in the eight corners formed by the structure of the ceiling. The usual Hindu method of construction is employed; thus across the corners of the outer four beams, slabs are laid cross-wise, forming an upper diagonal square. Above it a smaller square is set parallel to the beams, whose corners touch the centre of the sides of the diagonal. The triangular spaces have,—in addition to the central pateras—their surfaces covered with floral scrolls. The fronts of the triangular slabs are ornamented with floral scroll patterns. In the centre face of each, is a small square panel, having the regents of the eight cardinal points. Thus, the four regents of the intermediate points are on the centre of sides of the diagonal square; the remaining four are on the faces of the small upper square. The corona or centre-piece is a flat fluted circular dome with a moulded knob descending from the centre. Around it is a series of detached interlacing stems. Vyâli heads fill up the flat triangular surface between the upper square and the hollow circular dome.

Plate LIII.

Fig. 1.—A figure of Anantaśâyana in the temple of that name. He reclines on the coils of a Nâga, with the hoods of the snake shading his head. The pedestal of the image is a fine sharply cut example of Châlukyan moulded work.

Fig. 2.—The image in the shrine of Lakshmi-Narâyaṇasvâmi. Narâyaṇa is seated with Lakshmi on his left knee. Both figures are adorned with a profusion of finely cut ornaments. Overhead is a carved arched canopy, with open scroll work surmounted by figures of the fish and tortoise, and images representing the various gods. The group is placed on a pedestal, moulded almost precisely similar to that above described.

Fig. 3.—A sculptured panel over the shrine doorway of the Bhîmêśvera temple. In the centre is Îśvara, with Pârvati, and Gaṇapati and Subrahmaṇya on their right and left. Underneath Śiva, is his vehicle the bull. A female fan-bearer stands on each side of this central group.

On the right of the panel is Brahmâ with Sarasvati seated on his knee, and the vehicle of the former below.

On the left of the panel is Vishṇu, having Lakshmi seated on his knees. A fan-bearer is at the sides, and his vehicle, Garuḍa, underneath.

Each end of the panel is terminated by a makara, with a floral scroll springing from its tail.

Plate LIV.

Fig. 2.—The doorway to the central shrine. On each side of the door, separated by an ornamental pilaster and rows of floral ornament, is a perforated stone window, with three upright rows of floral scrolls. Each alternate scroll has a small figure seated inside. Under the door jambs and windows is a floral canopy covering three dvârapâlakas. The sill in front of these, is ornamented with a floral scroll. Outside each window is a finely moulded and carved semi-pier, with three dvârapâlakas under a canopy on the lower body of the shaft. The sculptured block, over the centre of the door soffit, represents Gajalakshmi. The frieze over the lintel has the usual group of the principal deities, with their wives, vehicles and attendants. The beam is moulded, and topped with notched crenellations.

Plate LV.

Figs. 1 and 2.—The front and side views of the sômasûtra for carrying off the pûja water from the shrine. This drainage channel, in the majority of temples, is usually comparatively plain. In a temple such as this, where carving is lavished wherever possible, it becomes a highly ornamental feature.

A makara head is at the end of the conduit which issues through the wall. In front of it is a short open channel, covered with a characteristic scroll ornament on both sides. The stone block on which it rests, has a makara on each side, and the rest of the surface covered with foliage.

A sômasûtra of similar design is seen at Mâgalâ.

Fig. 3.—A carved block surmounting a corner of the cornice.

CHAPTER VI.

KURUVATTI.

Malikârjuna Temple.

The village stands on the right bank of the Tuṅgabhadrâ river about 17 miles west of the taluk head-quarters of Harpanahaḷḷi.

The temple is said to have been formerly known by the name of Mallêśvara. The usual arrangement is observable in the plan, so that it will be sufficient if the chief features of variation are pointed out. (Pl. LVI.) The shrine has three interior niches in the thickness of the walls. The only other of these examples where this occurs, is at the Kêśavasvâmi temple at Huvinahaḍgalli, where there are two. The exterior shrine niches have considerable projection. Like the Kallêśvara temple at Huvinahaḍgalli, the shrine ante-chamber has side lights. In place of the usual entrance door to the ante-chamber, there is placed a finely sculptured pediment resting on columns. The front maṇḍapa has three doors; and the side porches have six columns each, instead of the more usual two.

The temple has only one shrine, at the west end, with a liṅga. A mask is fixed on the liṅga on festival occasions. On the floor in front of the shrine door is a finely carved scroll. On each side of the ante-chamber are two pilasters with figures of Vîrabhadra, Bhairava, Basava and two other images. The screen at the entrance to the ante-chamber has been above alluded to.

In the front maṇḍapa are four turned columns, with rectangular responding pilasters on the four walls. In the south-west corner is an inscribed stone, and images of Gaṇapati, and Sûrya Narâyaṇa.

In the south porch is a finely sculptured panel representing a Râjâ and two attendants with umbrellas. There are also three inscribed stones. These are not *in situ*, but have all been removed from some place in this or another building, and set down here. The doors of both the north and south porches are finely carved.

The east door also, is an exceedingly fine specimen. The base around the building has the usual members in its composition; numbers of the blocks on it are uncarved. The main wall is divided by a series of broad and narrow pilasters, with lesser ones between, some are single and others double; they support canopies and miniature reproductions of the main tower of the building itself. Each of the latter had at one time a projecting detached group of flying figures fixed in with sockets in the manner of those on the upper part of the front door, but now only the socket holes are left to indicate they have been there.

In the niches on the three faces of the shrine are various images. In that on the north, is Narasiṁha; on the east and south are images described as king Urduathandan and Bidehâdanar. (Pl. LVIII.) A photograph of a portion of this part of the building is shown in Mr. Fergusson's *Architecture in Dharwar and Mysore.* (Pl. XXXVI.) The ornaments of the wall-head cornice are in parts completely away, leaving only the rough masonry backing.

The lion is of frequent appearance in some of these temples, and in none more so than in this. It is shown in panels on the base, on wall-heads, angles of the tower, and other places. One is cut on the stylobate of a porch showing on plate LVII.

The shrine tower is complete, but disfigured by long repeated applications of whitewash. It is built in a series of recessed storeys, with unornamented horizontal mouldings. Two doors enter the tower over the roof of the front maṇḍapa. The Basava maṇḍapa opposite the temple is a modern building erected on ancient foundations. It is plain, with a tower over the shrine, and wooden pillars in the maṇḍapa in front.

Plate LIX.

Fig. 1.—One of the four central piers in the mahâmaṇḍapa. The column is circular moulded, without ornament on its upper portion. The base is square, with a representation of a shrine on each of the four faces. The beam brackets over the capital are plain.

Fig. 2.—One of the small niches on the outer walls. They are placed one on each side of the broad pilasters fixed at intervals on the sides and back of the temple. In place of an image, a small pilaster supporting a small tower stands inside.

Fig. 3.—One of the piers of the south porch. The plan of each, from base to capital, is a square, with notched corners.

Plate LX.

The east entrance to the mahâmaṇḍapa. This is a beautifully carved example of its class. The sculptured block in the centre of the lintel has the usual representation of Gaja-lakshmi. The covering cornice is plain, with miniature representations of towers over it. The jambs have an extra large number of upright rows of carvings. That next the door has diamond and floral patterns; the others are coiled Nâga figures, figure and bird scrolls dancers and musicians, a running scroll and a leaf patera. The figure scrolls and musicians are cut on the face of narrow pilasters which run up to the cornice over the door. The carving is generally deeply undercut and most minutely worked. Each group of figures differs in some respect from the others. Under each projection on the jambs, is a niche with a figure standing under a canopy, carved to represent a vimâna tower. Outside the jamb carvings is a massive flat pilaster with a double notch running up each corner. On the front and inner side of each capital are finely carved female figures with encircling wreaths (pl. LXVIII). This feature is unusual, and but seldom occurs in any of the present described group of Châlukyan temples. Another example occurs in the Kêśavasvâmi temple at Huvina-haḍgalli. In that building, only the supporting brackets remain. Each figure is supported on a bracket carved with a bhûta, fixed in the pilaster below the neck mouldings. The figures represent dancers, and each has some smaller figures of musicians at its feet. Around and down each side of the principal figure is a floral wreath. The figures and wreath are delicately and completely undercut as if carved in metal, and stand quite detached. They are as well finished on the back as on the front. A narrow slab of stone has been left on the back of each to give the necessary strength. The groups are on stones separate from the columns, and are held in position by an under pin fixed into the supporting bracket, and another upper one let into a projecting carved block overhead. Groups similar to these have been fixed in the niches on the sides of the temple, but are now away. Enlarged drawings of two of these groups are shown on plate LXVIII.

Plate LXI.

A niche and adjoining portion of the exterior wall on the south side of the shrine. There is a similar niche on the centre of the back, and the north side. The niche is surmounted by a heavy cornice and a miniature shrine tower. A deity sits inside the niche—in this instance Narasiṁha. The base is flanked by elephants. On each side is a bhûta figure-bracket, which originally supported flying groups of figures, which leant forward and were fitted into the underside of the cornice. They were similar to those on the upper sides of the front door. Being so close to the ground, they have been interfered with, become loose in their sockets, and either fallen or been taken out. One of those from the niche under note has been preserved, and is now in the Government Museum at Madras.

Plate LXII.

Fig. 1.—A finely carved toran standing in the mahâmaṇḍapa, in front of the doorway which leads into the shrine. It is formed of two circular moulded Châlukyan piers supporting a large pediment or lintel. The principal features in the structure are the three deities standing in the carved niches under a semi-circular arch which is pierced through the slab. These represent Śiva in the centre, with Brahmâ on his right and Vishṇu on his left. At each side of the arch is a makara with figures seated on its back. From its mouth springs an ornament which goes round the arch and terminates in a vyâli head. From the tail, a profusion of floral ornament curves out, and fills up the sides of the slab. The back of the slab is plain.

Fig. 2.—A carved centre block representing Gajalakshmi on the lintel of the south doorway.

Fig. 3.—A carved wooden doorway in the Basava maṇḍapa. The design is a series of pateras in panels up each jamb and along the lintel.

Figs. 4 and 5.—Ornaments on the east and south doors.

Plate LXIII.

Figs. 1 to 4.—Door architrave ornaments. Fig. 1, is a scroll with figures, from the north door. Fig. 2, is another of the upright bands of ornament from the same door. Figs. 3 and 4, are lozenge and scroll ornaments from the east door.

Fig. 5.—A mantram, or charm to ward off disease from cattle, cut on a stone standing in the small village of Katibinuru.

Plate LXIV.

Fig. 1.—A beaten brass mask for fitting on to the liṅga on festival occasions. The body of the figure represents the head of Śiva with the head of Gaṅga in his crown. Around the base are the coils of a Nâga, whose outspread hood overshadows the liṅga.

Fig. 2.—A cast brass image of Śiva, with Pârvati, seated on his vehicle Nandi, and overshadowed by a five-hooded Nâga. Behind him is a canopy supported on two piers. Over the arch of the canopy are four banners and an umbrella in silver. Enlarged drawings of these silver ornaments are shown in plate LXVII, figs. 1 to 3. These latter are included in the *Technical Art Series*, 1891.

Plate LXV.

Fig. 1.—A beaten brass head for fitting on to the liṅga. It is cylinder-shaped, with an ornamental dome-shaped head-piece. On the front is a mask or face. Each of the ears has a karnapushpam or wing-shaped ornament attached.

Fig. 2.—A sculptured stone lying in a road in the village. It is in the style of, and has probably been taken from the temple there. The subject is Gajalakshmi. It is rather curiously treated. Two elephants stand grasping water-pots with their trunks, while other two stand on their backs and pour the contents of their pots over the goddess. At each side is the head of a makara devouring a ram.

Fig. 3.—The floral canopy and miniature tower over one of the side wall niches.

Fig. 4.—A carved ornament on the chief entrance door jamb.

Plate LXVI.

Fig. 1.—A finely sculptured slab standing in the south porch. It represents Îśvara seated under triple umbrellas, and accompanied by his wives and female attendants. The image is not now in its original position.

Fig. 2.—An *alto-relievo* of Nârâyaṇasvâmi, standing in the mahâmaṇḍapa.

Plate LXVII.

Figs. 1, 2 and 3, are the silver banners and umbrella referred to in the description of plate LXIV, fig. 2.

Fig. 4.—A silver waist belt. It is of modern make, and is similar to those generally worn by Kanarese women in this part of the country. It is made of pure or nearly pure silver. The girth is arranged by increasing or lessening the undulations at the back. The front panels pivot on the dividing pins. One of the pins in front screws out to allow of the belt being put on.

Fig. 5.—A carved slab lying in a road of the village. It is one of the blocks usually placed at the side of entrance steps. It is in the same style of art as the temple, and may have been taken from it. It is very boldly carved. On one side is a lion, with a floral scroll flowing from its mouth. In the scrolls are small human figures. An elephant is being crushed beneath one of the front paws of the lion. The lion's tail and raised forepaw have been carved so as to be almost quite detached from the slab and are now broken away. The upper part of a man who stands in front, is, for the same reason, also broken off.

Plate LXVIII.

Figs. 1 and 2, are the two flying figure-brackets referred to in the description of plate LX. One is illustrated in Mr. Fergusson's *Architecture of Dharwar and Mysore*, plate XXXVII.

CHAPTER VII.

HUVINAHAḌGALLI.

Kallêśvara Temple.

The head quarters of the taluk of that name, standing 67 miles west of the town of Ballâri.

The plan of the temple (pl. LXIX) consists of a square shrine and an enclosed mahâmaṇḍapa, separated from each other by a small ante-chamber. The shrine has a series of rectangular projections on the centre of each exposed face, and another at each corner. The exterior walls of the mahâmaṇḍapa show an enlargement of the same arrangement. This building has a front and a side porch entrance; the latter is now blocked up with a mud wall. In the centre of the floor is a slightly raised platform on which stand four circular moulded piers (pl. LXX). Two responding pilasters are in the centre of each of the four walls. The central compartment of the ceiling is circular moulded, with a leaf ornament on each of the rings. It is much less ornate than the ceilings generally found in this position in other temples of this class of building; as at Mâgalâ for example.

The small ante-chamber is lighted by an open rectangular window on each side, into the sill of which, a carved upright stone was fixed. (Plate LXXI.) The room has a plain ceiling of a not unusual pattern composed of slabs laid to form a diagonal, square, and circle. Its entrance door (Plate LXX) is comparatively plain, with perforated panels at each side and over the lintel. In front of it reclines a Nandi, facing the shrine.

The front and side doors are both of similar design, the former being the more ornamental. The style of the exterior can best be judged, by a reference to the various drawings of the elevations. (Plates LXXI, LXXII and LXXIII.) The wall is divided by a series of narrow pilasters with projecting niches at intervals. A figure of a lion over an elephant is in a panel on one side. (Plate LXXI.)

The tower which surmounts the shrine is ruined at the summit. Various pieces of ornament from the different parts of the building, to illustrate its style, are separately shown.

Plate LXXIV.

The doorway in the blocked up south porch. It is similar in design to that at the front entrance door; only in that instance the lower architrave mouldings are stopped by the plinth of the porch, which projects on each side. The design and application of the various ornaments do not materially differ from others elsewhere described in detail. The various points of difference can best be seen by a comparison with other examples illustrated. The door has no heavy cornice over. The upper mouldings and ornament bear a general resemblance to those on the wall head cornice of the temple.

Plate LXXV.

The central bay of the back exterior wall of the shrine. The small niche with miniature tower over, is repeated at intervals along the walls. Some have a small figure standing inside; others have none. Groups of various animals, similar to those appearing here, are placed along the cornice. The ornaments over, are likewise carried around. Between the small projecting blocks carved with a makara head, a carved cross-shaped ornament may be specially noted. It appears on the other cornices of the tower and also on the base. The carved panel surmounting the cornice, is another feature that has been placed on the wall-head over the principal projections; but only a few of them now remain.

Plate LXXVI.

Fig. 1.—One of the piers in the south porch, an entrance now blocked up with mud walls. Its plan is square, with notched corners. There are two piers in the porch. The one here illustrated, is shorter in the plinth than the other, through a parapet wall running against it.

Fig. 2.—A detail drawing of the mouldings and ornament of the main base of the building.

Plate LXXVII.

Fig. 1.—The ornament on the main base.

Figs. 2 to 5.—Images on slabs standing near the adjoining tank. They respectively represent Ganêśa, a Nâga, Kâlabhairava, and Nârâyaṇa.

Plate LXXVIII.

Fig. 1.—One of the two pilasters at the side of the door connecting the mahâmaṇḍapa with the shrine. There are two pilasters on the centre of each of the inner faces of this building, but they are of different design. A reference to the section will show their position (plate LXX).

Fig. 2.—A pilaster in the south porch.

Plate LXXIX.

(Ornaments on cornices on the tower.)

Fig. 1 is the drop ornament on the face of the main cornice over the upper storey. The small figure block is placed on each projection.

Fig. 2.—The cornice over the first storey above the wall-head of the shrine.

Plate LXXX.

Fig. 1.—A cornice ornament on the tower.

Fig. 2.—A sculptured slab standing in the road near the temple.

Plate LXXXI.

A cornice and ornament on the tower.

Plate LXXXII.

Figs. 1 and 2.—Details of the lower part of the tower where it rises from the roof of the temple. The mouldings, and ornaments over the pilasters, form the string courses which run round this portion of the tower. The surmounting terminal is one of those fixed at intervals over this series of mouldings.

Plate LXXXIII.

One of the triple carved panel blocks which are placed in the centre of each storey of the tower. The central panel has a figure of Narasiṁha; a female chauri bearer stands in each of the side panels.

Plate LXXXIV.

Fig. 1.—A carved panel block on the wall-head; with a deity and his two wives in the central panel, and a female fan bearer in each of the side panels.

Fig. 2.—A cornice ornament in the form of a floral cross, having a makara head and and animal with the body of a lion and the head of an elephant.

Plate LXXXV.

Figs. 1 and 2.—Ornamental blocks surmounting the parapets of the wall-head. Fig. 1 is an example of those at the corners. Fig. 2 is one surmounting a pilaster. The upper part is stepped, and crowned with a vyâli head, from which drops the ornament decorating the block. The centre generally has either a circular lotus or other floral design, or a figure of a deity.

Plate LXXXVI.

Figs. 1 and 2 are ornamental blocks over the corners of the parapet, similar to those above described.

Plate LXXXVII.

An ornamental slab over the cornice on the north side. On the cornice are various figures standing in relief. The lower part of the slab has projecting marks in the form of makaras' heads, similar to those on the main base of the building. The upper triangular panel has a vyâli's head with flowers springing from the mouth.

Plate LXXXVIII.

The plate shows a pilaster on the exterior of the wall, with the upper members of the base and wall-head cornice. The opening in the wall is the window which lights the shrine ante-chamber.

Plate LXXXIX.

Fig. 1.—The Nandi standing in the mahâmaṇḍapa facing the shrine entrance. The base mouldings of the pedestal have been somewhat mutilated. The animal and pedestal are cut in one block of blackstone.

Fig. 2.—Haṁsa ornament on the main cornice.

Plate XC.

Fig. 1.—A carved panel in the wall over the gateway of the fort. It has evidently been taken from some other building and placed there. In the floral canopy which surmounts the figure, birds and monkeys are seen plucking the bunches of fruit.

Figs. 2 and 3.—Two Nâga stones at the temple.

Plate XCI.

A terminal member over groups of pilasters on the tower.

CHAPTER VIII.

HUVINAHAḌGALLI.

KÊŚAVASVÂMI TEMPLE.

The plan of this building, in general outline, resembles that of the Śiva temple of Kallêśvara. On examination however, a number of points of difference can be noted. (Pl. XCII.) The exterior central niches of the shrine are wider and have a greater projection. There are also two interior niches in the walls. The ante-chamber has no side lights. There are three doors to the mahâmaṇḍapa. One of the side doors has a projecting porch, while the other has a sort of interior vestibule formed in the thickness of the wall.

The style of work on the exterior is radically different from the other. (Pls. XCIII and XCIV.) The base blocks are uncarved. The jamb and lintel bands of the doors are in the same condition, though it is evident that the original intention was to have them carved.

The wall pilasters are of broad and narrow pattern. The former somewhat resemble those at Kuruvatti.

On the wall-heads are rough stone walls. These seem to be the solid masonary backing to the carved and moulded cornice blocks, which however, are now all away. Parts of the temple at Kuruvatti are in a similar condition, though not so completely denuded of everything carved. (Compare Pls. LVII, LVIII.) No trace of any shrine tower exists. The temple is covered with whitewash.

Several pieces of carving and sculpture, probably taken from this temple, are lying at various places in the neighbourhood.

A short distance away, are three small blackstone temples. They are all whitewashed. A doorway from one of them, the Kṛishṇadêva temple, with carved panels over, and perforated windows and panels over is shown on plate XCV.

PLATE XCV.

The shrine doorway; as is sometimes the case with doors in this position, it has a perforated window on each side. In this example, the lights also, are carried right across the top. There is no cornice, but the lintel is deep, and highly carved. The usual central block with Gajalakshmi does not find a place here. The carving on the lintel, in design resembles that found at a door at Bâgali; in that however, the feature is not on the lintel, but over the cornice. (Pl. V, fig. 2) The present example has no dvârapâlakas; under the window sills are figures seated in a panel, with pilasters and floral-cusped arches. Figures are also seated in the panels on the face of the door step.

PLATE XCVI.

Fig. 1.—One of the central piers in the mahâmaṇḍapa. The base is square, with the usual carvings found on piers standing in this position. The shaft is round, with a square abacus.

Fig. 2. —A slab standing at the tank. The image is Yôganarasiṁha.

Fig. 3. —A slab at the same place carved with Ganêśa.

Plate XCVII.

The image in the shrine. It is less highly carved, and has not the profusion of jewellery usually seen on the images in the temples under note.

Plate XCVIII.

One of the niches on the walls. The lower part of the base is covered with an accumulation of soil. The work is devoid of sculpture with the exception of the bhûta figure brackets on the pilasters. These have evidently supported flying figures similar to those at Kuruvatti.

Plate XCIX.

Fig. 1.—A liṅga in the temple at the tank.

Figs. 2 and 3.—Nâga and Nâgakanya stones at the same place.

Fig. 4.—A figure bracket on the wall of the Kêśavasvâmi temple.

Plate C.

Fig. 1.—A good example of an inscribed Nâgakal standing in a field a short distance east of the Kallêśvara temple.

Fig. 2.—An ornamental band under the necking of the piers of the side porch.

Plate CI.

Fig. 1.—A panelled niche on the wall of the temple of Hanumân, with figures of Nâgêndra and Nâgakanya.

Figs. 2 and 3.—Ornaments on the jamb of the east doorway of the same temple.

CHAPTER IX.

HALAVÂGALU.

Kallêśvara Temple.

A village, 13 miles west by south of the taluk head-quarters of Harpanahaḷḷi.

The plan of the temple is that of an undeveloped three-shrined building. (Pl. CII.) The door to the hall enters on one side; a shrine enters off each of the others. Only one of the shrines has an open ante-chamber; the others have none; or, at least, what are now enclosed and used as shrines, may have originally been intended as ante-chambers to cells which would have stood outside them. In the main shrine is a liṅga with a brass five-headed Nâgêndra encircling it. In the centre shrine, opposite the doorway, is a stone figure of Kêśavasvâmi; in the other are an inscribed stone and some Nâgakals.

Four massive and plainly moulded piers stand in the central hall or mahâmaṇḍapa.

There is an almost complete absence of carved work in the temple, though the rough blocks at the doors show that it had been intended to sculpture them. The only carved ceiling is that in the central compartment of the hall; it has a simple lotus leaf patera.

A Gaṇêśa stands inside the hall, and some sculptured stones outside the entrance. A modern maṇḍapa has been erected in front. The walls are blocked up by houses. There is no detail on the exterior.

Plate CIII.

Fig. 1.—A pier in the temple. It has a square moulded base with a plain block on the centre of each of the faces. The shaft is square, with two sixteen-sided fluted sections divided by octagonal bands in the middle of the length. The capital is circular moulded, with four brackets above. The pier is of a type commonly met with in temples of subsequent date in some parts of these districts, and represents a combination of Châlukyan and Dravidian forms in its design.

Fig. 2.—A figure of Vishṇu in the shrine of Kêśavasvâmi of the Kallêśvara temple. He is placed on a moulded pedestal under a carved canopy. At his feet stand his two wives.

Plate CIV.

One of the slabs standing at the entrance door. The lower panel has a leader on horse-back, attended by an umbrella bearer, with his soldiers behind, attacking a number of other horsemen. Soldiers are seen advancing on the heads and shoulders of dwarfs.

The panel over, has three figures engaged in worship in a small shrine. They may represent the chief and his two wives. Three figures are on each side of the exterior.

The top panel represents the worship of the liṅga by three figures seated on one side, and other two figures, one of whom waves a lamp in the right hand and bears some offering in the other. The sun and moon; and a finial, in the form of a vase, surmount the stone.

PLATE CV.

Fig. 1.—A monumental slab with three panels. The lower panel represents a fighting scene. A foot warrior armed with sword (or spear ?) and shield carries all before him. He is shown as attacking a horse, whose rider seems in the act of losing his seat. Another horse is riderless, and the opposing footmen are being trampled under his own and the horse's feet.

The panel over, has five figures with their arms linked round each other's necks and waists. It does not seem exactly clear whether they are engaged in dancing to celebrate a victory, or the wounded being carried off the field by the two figures on each side of him.

The top panel shows a rude liṅga.

Fig. 2 is one of a similar class of carved slabs, very much dilapidated.

Fig. 3 is another of these monumental slabs with a spirited fighting scene in the lowest panel.

CHAPTER X.

HARIHAR.

HARIHARÊŚVARA TEMPLE.

A village in Maisûr territory, standing 14 miles south of Halavâgalu. Owing to its close position to the group of temples, to the illustration of which this volume is devoted, and as it presents some features which can with advantage be compared with them, a plan (Pl. CVI), and some details have been included. The arrangement of plan, it will be seen, most closely resembles Bâgali. The main shrine in this case is typically Châlukyan.

PLATE CVII.

A flat ceiling in the antarâla maṇḍapa. It is divided by four cross ribs into nine panels. In the centre panel is Îśvara standing in a niche surrounded by various small images. The remaining eight panels represent the Ashtadik-pâlakas or regents of the eight cardinal points. Each is there, mounted on his vehicle.

The Ashtadik-pâlakas are thus given in Ziegenbalg's *South Indian Gods*, pp. 8, 191.

No.	*Name.*	*Regent of*	*Vehicle.*
1	Indra.	East.	Elephant.
2	Agni.	South-east.	Gray goat.
3	Yama.	South.	Black buffalo.
4	Niruti.	South-west.	Crocodile.
5	Varuṇa.	West.	Stag.
6	Vâyu.	North-west.	Bhûta.
7	Kuvêra.	North.	Self-moving chariot.
8	Îśâna.	North-east.	Bull.

It will be observed that in a few cases the vehicles, shown in this plate, differ from those above quoted. Thus No. 4 has a bhûta instead of a crocodile; No. 5 a crocodile instead of a stag; No. 6 a stag instead of a bhûta; and No. 7 a horse instead of a self-moving chariot.

If these in this plate are compared with those in another shown elsewhere, (Pl. II, fig. 1) it will be seen that, except in two instances, they correspond. Thus in the last, No. 2 has a horse instead of a goat; and No. 7 has a goat instead of a horse. The three may thus be summarised for easy comparison.

Vehicles of the Ashtadik-pâlakas.

No.	*Ziegenbalg.*	*Plate CVII.*	*Plate II.*
1	Elephant.	Elephant.	Elephant.
2	Gray goat.	Gray goat.	Horse.
3	Black buffalo.	Black buffalo.	Black buffalo.
4	Crocodile.	Bhûta.	Bhûta.
5	Stag.	Crocodile.	Crocodile.
6	Bhûta.	Stag.	Stag.
7	Chariot.	Horse.	Gray goat.
8	Bull.	Bull.	Bull.

PLATE CVIII.

The central ceiling in the Amman shrine of the temple. This is one of the finest pieces of black stone carving in the temple. No drawing can ever do justice to the splendidly rich effect it has in reality. In plan it is a square of four beams with triangular blocks placed over the corners, forming an octagon, on which rests a circular dome. The dome is constructed of large horizontal blocks. Its entire inner surface is moulded into different sections, and profusely covered with rich and varied ornament. From the central coping stone descends a deep ornamental circular pendant.

On each under side of the beams, over the capitals of the piers, is a raised circular patera. Smaller pateras are on the triangular blocks at the corners. On the centre of the faces of these blocks and on the inner faces of the four beams are plain square blocks, eight in all. It was doubtless intended that these should be carved with the Ashtadik-pâlakas or regents of the eight cardinal points, and protectors of the earth, as is usual in such works.

In the circular dome, the first course is plainly moulded. The next has leaves radiating from the centre. Over is a cavetto, divided by closely placed vertical bands, into panels with a small patera in each. A small fillet over, has its under side covered with small rosettes. The upper courses are ornamented with interlaced semi-circles, filled in with various designs between.

The under faces of the mouldings of the pendant have interlacing semi-circles, trefoils, pateras, and other ornaments. The side faces have various floral designs. There is a ceiling similar to this, in the mahâmaṇḍapa of the Kallêśvara temple at Bâgali.

Plate CIX.

Figs. 1 and 2.—One of two dîpastambhas at the east gate. This particular form of lamp-pillar is peculiar to these districts, and is not found further south. The ordinary dîpdân with lamps on the top only, exists all over the Presidency. Good examples are seen at Vijayanagar.

The present example is comparatively modern, having been built within the past century. It however, in no wise differs from more ancient examples found elsewhere. The shaft is octagonal with a very decided taper towards the top. It is built in courses, and thus presents another difference to the ordinary dîpdân. Lamp-brackets project in rows, on the different faces alternately from base to capital.

Fig. 3.—The image of Kâlabhairava in the shrine devoted to its worship.

Fig. 4.—A monumental slab standing near the svâmi shrine. It differs from others elsewhere described as being at Halavâgalu, in that it has five panels, while those at that place have three. The lowest panel shows a bowman on foot, followed by two horses, slaughtering some foot soldiers. The next seems to be a scene of rejoicing, five figures being engaged in dancing. In the third panel, a figure sits inside and two others outside a small antique shrine. The piers and pent roof of slabs, are similar to a small temple at Bâgali. (Pl. III.) In the fourth panel side figures seem engaged in the act of supporting and bearing off another in the centre. The top panel has a liṅga and worshipper. The two top dividing bands have inscriptions. One half of the top of the slab is broken away.

Fig. 5.—A carved architrave on the door illustrated on plate CXI.

Plate CX.

A flat panelled ceiling in the mahâmaṇḍapa, divided by ribs into six panels. The ribs are ornamented on their under sides with a flowing scroll, and their angles have a moulded ornamental chamfer. In each panel is a large circular concave patera, divided into concentric bands of ornament, with a drop in the centre. Four of the pateras have simple circles of radiating leaves. The other two have circles of small sunk ornamental panels. The four main beams enclosing the ceiling, have notched crenellations, and miniature pilasters or balusters, with leaf ornament between.

Plate CXI.

Fig. 1.—Elevation of the north wall of the shrine at the north-east corner. The lower plinth of the base has a floral scroll with figures. Above is a row of haṁsas or sacred geese. The main base has the usual series of sharply cut mouldings surmounted by a cyma recta coping. The main walls are divided into compartments by pilasters running from the base to the cornice. In each of these panels is a niche with pilasters and cornice, surmounted by a miniature representation of a shrine tower. The texture of the blackstone admits of its being cut into the most minute mouldings, and each of these is cut and finished as if it had been wrought in ivory. The usual cornice surmounts the walls. Over it is an ornamental parapet with lions carved on blocks, and a coping ornamented at intervals with carved blocks enclosing small figures.

Fig. 2.—The carved door of the Kâlabhairava shrine. The architrave around the opening has one row of flat diagonal diapers, and another of convex section with figure and floral scrolls. These are shown to an enlarged scale in fig. 5, of plate CIX. On each side is a moulded pilaster with its corners stepped off for the entire height. Outside are a vertical row of scrolls of convex section, and leaves coiled around a stem. The five different members, on each side of the door, are separated by a deep groove, with small blocks left at intervals in the height. Below the pilasters and upright ornaments, are niches with ornamental canopy enclosing a figure. Gajalakshmi, with an inscription below, is in a carved panel on a block over the centre of the doorway.

Plate CXII.

Fig. 1.—The image of Hariharêśwara in the shrine. It is a stiffly carved figure, nearly devoid of ornament. A peculiar feature is seen in two of the arms resting on side piers brought up to support them. The legs too, from the knees downwards, are hidden behind a plinth. These have not been part of the image originally, but are ingenious devices to conceal and remedy a defect or fracture of the arms and legs.

Figs. 2 to 4.—Sculptured details on the basement wall around the mahâmaṇḍapa. Fig. 2 shows a line of haṁsas or sacred geese. Fig. 3 is a row of elephants and horses. The former as usual, are more true to life than the latter, which are stiff and ungraceful. Fig. 4 has a floral scroll with figures inside.

Plate CXIII.

Fig. 1.—A characteristic ornamental architrave up the side of the door of the east entrance to the mahâmaṇḍapa. One row is a wide scroll with images and foliage alternately. In the middle row, is a narrow floral scroll. The outer line has a row of diapers.

Fig. 2.—A horizontal scroll on the front entrance to the mahâmaṇḍapa.

Fig. 3.—One of the piers of the extensive colonnade in the mahâmaṇḍapa. The base is square, with the usual Châlukyan mouldings for this member. These are a moulding in the centre, with a fillet on the front, and a splay on both sides. Lower and upper splays, with small fillets, separate the central member from a lower plinth or broad fillet, and another fillet or tenia on the top.

The lower part of the column is square, the upper part circular, with the usual minute finely cut mouldings; and the abacus square with notched corners. Above the abacus, four moulded and ornamental consoles, with a notched block in front of each, support the four cross beams of the ceiling. An ovolo moulding, with a stop ornament at the extremities, runs along the edges of the beams.

Fig. 4.—A pier in the east gate. This style of pier is of a peculiar class, differing considerably from the more usual pier found in mahâmaṇḍapas and other interior parts of the main building, such as that in fig. 3. It is similar to others in the porches of the Jaina temples at Hampi in Vijayanagar. When used, it is generally seen in such outer buildings as porches or gates. It has no base, the square under portion of the pier resting directly on the floor. The upper and main body of the shaft is fluted in sixteen sides, with a row of plain leaves at the lower extremity. The necking is plain, and circular. The capital is a flattened disc with a fillet on the edge, and rows of minute fillets and flutes underneath, resembling those under the ovolo of the Grecian Doric capital.

A square block rests on the convex upper surface of the capital, whose four corners almost touch its outer circumference. Above this, are four consoles supporting the beams, of a design almost precisely similar to those of fig. 3.

CHAPTER XI.

BIDRAHAḶḶI FORT.

Plate CXIV.

This is a village in Bombay territory on the bank of the Tuṅgabhadrâ river, opposite Mûgalâ. The temple is a small Châlukyan structure standing in the fort.

Fig. 1.—A pâñchâyatana or liṅga with five heads, lying in the courtyard with its parivattam buried in the ground. The heads represent the five faces of Siva, of whom the liṅga is the symbol; they are variously named :—

1.—Sûryôjâta, or Âdityâ.
2.—Vâmadêvam, „ Aṁbika.
3.—Aghôram, „ Śiva.
4.—Tatpurusham, „ Basavanna.
5.—Îśa, „ Pârvati.

Fig. 2.—A Châlukyan pier. Its detail is similar to that found in piers in temples of the date in the adjoining districts of Ballâri. The capital, however, with the acanthus-shaped leaves, does not occur in any of the others.

APPENDIX.

GLOSSARY OF INDIAN NAMES.

Adityâ. The sun.

Aghôram. A terrible form of Îśvara or Śiva.

Agni. The god of fire, and regent of the south-east.

Airâvata. The white elephant of Indra.

Ambika. A goddess.

Amman. Goddess.

Anantapûr. The principal town in the district of the same name.

Anantaśâyana. Vishṇu reclining on the serpent.

Antarâlamaṇḍapa. The ante-chamber in front of a shrine.

Apsaras. Heavenly maidens.

Ardhamaṇḍapa. The enclosed building in front of a shrine.

Ashtadikpâlakas. The regents of the eight cardinal points.

Asura, or Râkshasa. The enemy of the gods: descended from the Rishi Kâśyapa.

Avatâr. An incarnation.

Bâgali. A village in the Ballâri district.

Ballâḷas. A dynasty ruling in Maisûr, from the beginning of the eleventh to the beginning of the fourteenth century. The style of architecture found in their temples is a variety of the Châlukyan.

Ballâri. The principal town in the district of the same name.

Basappa. Basava, or Basavanna. The Canarese name of Nandi, the bull vehicle of Śiva (and also of the fierce Vîra-Śaiva).

Bhairava. A terrible form of Śiva.

Bhîmêśvara. One of the five Pâṇḍavas; a man of great strength.

Bhûta. A demon; dwarf.

Bidchâdanar. Incarnation as a beggar.

Bidrahaḷḷi. A village on the banks of the Tuṅgabhadrâ river, opposite Mâgalâ.

Brahmâ. One of the Mummûrtis, viz., the creator; one of the five faces of Śiva.

Buddhist architecture in the south, is represented by examples dating from the third century B.C., to the fifth century A.D.

Châlukyas. A dynasty first heard of in the sixth and reigning till the twelfth century. The style of architecture herein illustrated, is named after them, though it was also practised by others than they.

Châna. Good; beautiful.

Chauri. A fan usually made of a yak's tail, used by attendants on the gods.

Chôḷas. A dynasty who reigned over a great portion of the south, and reached their greatest power about the eleventh century. Many examples of their temples of that date still exist. The principal example is the temple at Tañjâvûr (Tanjore). Their architecture is distinctive, and succeeds that of the Pallavas.

Dêvêndra or Indra. The king of the Dêvas, the regent of the east.

Dharmâveram. One of the principal towns in the Anantapûr district.

Dharwar. A town and district in the south of the Bombay presidency.

Dîpdân. A lamp pillar. In the south, it is usually a high monolith, with an iron lamp bracket on the top. In the north-west of the presidency, they are sometimes constructed in courses, with lamp brackets in the joints. The pillars are erected outside the front entrance.

Dîpastambha. A small lamp pillar, standing inside the temple.

Dravidian. Drâvida; or South-Indian.

Durga. A form of Pàrvati, and one of the Gràmadêvatas (village deities).

Dvàrapâlakas. Door-keepers; in temples, they are represented by sculptured figures on the door jambs.

Gaja Lakshmi. A favourite sculptured representation of Vishṇu's wife with elephants on each side, found on door lintels.

Gaṇapati. The belly god; the elephant-headed son of Śiva.

Ganêśa. Lord of hosts; another name of Vighnêśvara or Gaṇapati.

Gaṅga. The river Ganges; Îśvara's second wife.

Garuḍa. The kite; Vishṇu's vehicle.

Haidarabâd. Principal town in the State of that name.

Halavàgalu. A village in the Ballàri district.

Hampi. One of the villages at Vijayanagar in the Ballâri district.

Haṁsas. Celestial geese.

Hanumân. The monkey general, who assisted Ràma in his war with Ràvaṇa, being regarded and worshipped as a demi-god.

Harihar. A village in Maisûr.

Harihareśvara. Śiva.

Harpanahaḷḷi. A village in the Ballâri district.

Hirahaḍagalli. A village in the Ballàri district.

Hiraṇyakasipu. A râkshasa king destroyed by Vishṇu as Narasiṁha.

Hitadêvaru. Beloved god.

Holâlu. A village in the Ballàri district.

Hoyśala Ballâḷas. See Ballâḷas.

Huvinahaḍgalli. A village in the Ballàri district.

Indra. See Dêvêndra.

Îśa. Literally lord; generally applied to Śiva.

Îśàna. The regent of the north-east; a form of Îśvara.

Îśvara. Identical with Śiva, one of the Trimûrtis.

Jaina architecture. A style resembling in some of its features, that known as Châlukyan.

Kàlabhairava. Identical with Yama; the king of death and hell.

Kalaśa. A term applied generally to the summit of a tower; also a pot or vessel with water and some grains in it.

Kallêśvara. A deity; a form of Śiva.

Kaṁbadûru. A village in the Anantapûr district.

Karnapushpam. A wing-shaped ornament.

Katibinuru. A village in the Ballàri district.

Kattêśvara. A deity; a form of Śiva.

Kêśavasvàmi. One of the names of Vishṇu.

Kṛishṇa, Kṛishṇadêva or Kṛishṇasvâmi. The eighth incarnation of Vishṇu.

Kuruvatti. A village in the Ballàri district.

Kuvêra. The god of riches; the regent of the north.

Lakshmi. The chief wife of Vishṇu.

Lakshmi Nàrâyaṇasvâmi. Vishṇu with Lakshmi seated on his thigh.

Liṅga. The principal form under which Śiva is worshipped.

Madapalli. A cooking-room.
Mâgalâ. A village in the Ballâri district.
Mahâmaṇḍapa. The great hall of entrance to the main shrine of a temple.
Mahishâsura. A buffalo-headed giant.
Mahishâsuramardini. The goddess who slew Mahishâsura.
Maisûr. Province of Maisûr in Southern India.
Makra or Makara. A crocodile; also an ear ornament made of flowers.
Malikârjuna. A name of Śiva.
Mallêśvara. A deity; a form of Śiva.
Maṇḍapa. Any open or enclosed building in connection with a temple. If used for any special purpose, the distinctive name is prefixed.
Mantram. A charm. Formulæ of prayer, supposed to have a magic power.
Musalmân. Muhammadan.

Nâga. Serpent.
Nâgakal. A stone on which the image of a serpent is carved.
Nâgakanya. Serpent goddess.
Nâgêndra. Lord of serpents.
Nandi. The bull of Śiva or Îśvara.
Narasiṁha or Narasiṁhasvâmi. Vishṇu's incarnation as the man-lion.
Narâyaṇadêva or Narâyaṇasvâmi. Identical with Vishṇu.
Navagaṇas. The nine celestials.
Nilaguṇḍa. A village in the Ballâri district.
Niruti. A giant; the regent of the south-west.

Pallava. A dynasty of kings who had their capital at Kâñchîvaram in the eleventh century. They were a powerful race many centuries anterior to that date. Their architecture is distinctive. It succeeded that of the Buddhists. Examples date from the fifth to the seventh centuries. They include the remains at Mâmallapuram (Seven Pagodas) among the most important; and other structural and cave temples in various parts of the presidency.
Pâñchâyatana. A liṅga with five heads.
Parivattam. An arch like construction: a canopy.
Pârvati. The consort of Îśvara or Śiva.
Pârvatîsamêtha. Śiva in company with Pârvati, his faithful consort.
Prahlâda. A devotee of Vishṇu, saved from the hands of Hiraṇya by Vishṇu in his incarnation as Narasiṁha.
Pûja. Worship with ceremonies.

Râjâ. King.
Râkshasas. Savages; enemies of the gods; see Asura.
Râma. An incarnation of Vishṇu as the son of King Dasaratha of Ayôdhya (Oude).

Śaktis. Wives; the female power of the Supreme Being.
Sangan Basappa. A bull incarnation.
Sarasvati. The consort of Brahmâ; and the goddess of letters.
Śikara. Applied to the summit of a tower.
Sitêśvara. Râma; husband of Sita.
Siva. One of the Trimûrtis; the Supreme Being.
Śivaskandavarman. An early Pallava king.
Sôgi. A village in the Ballâri district.
Sòmasûtra. The drainage channel from the shrine; an ornamental feature on these temples.
Subrahmaṇya. Îśvara's younger son.
Sûrya-Narâyaṇa, or Sûrya Narâyaṇasvâmi. The sun.

Suryôjâta. One of the five faces of Śiva.

Svâmi. God; lord; applied to any of the gods, and usually affixed to their names.

Tatpurusham. The Supreme Being.

Toran. A structure formed of one or more horizontal beams resting on columns; a gateway or other detached entrance.

Trimurti. The Hindu triad: Śiva, Brahmâ, and Vishṇu.

Tuṅgabhadrà. A tributary of the Kṛishṇa river.

Urduathandan. The name of a king.

Vaishnavas. Followers of Vishṇu.

Vâmadêvam. One of the five faces of Śiva.

Varuṇa The regent of the west, and the god of waters.

Vâyu. The regent of the north-west and the god of winds.

Veṇugopàlasvàmi. Kṛishṇa with a lute.

Vijayanagar. The ancient capital of the kingdom of the name.

Vimâna. The tower of a shrine.

Vìrabhadra. A terrible being, created by Śiva for the purpose of destroying the sacrifice of Daksha.

Vìrakal. A stone erected in memory of a fallen warrior.

Vìrubakshi. A mythical bird.

Vishṇu. The Supreme Being; one of the Hindu triad.

Vishṇappa. An appellation of Vishṇu.

Vyâlis. Grotesque lion-like carvings.

Yàli. See vyâlis.

Yama. The king of death and hell, and regent of the south.

Yògaṇarasiṁha. Narasiṁha performing asceticism.

PLATE I

BAGALI: KALLESVARA TEMPLE.

Plan.

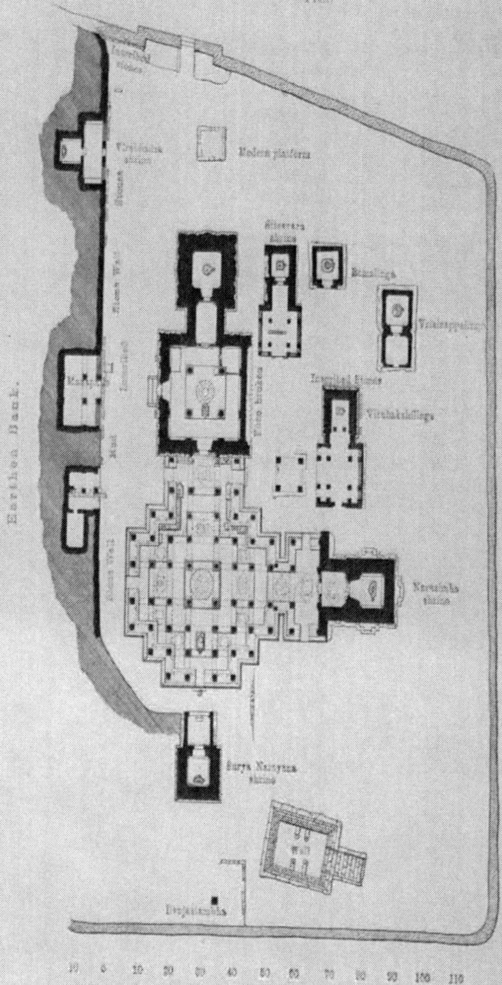

Photo-print, Survey Office, Madras.

PLATE III

BAGALI. CHANA BASAVA AND KALLESVARA TEMPLES.

Chana Basava Temple.

Fig. 2. Ground plan.

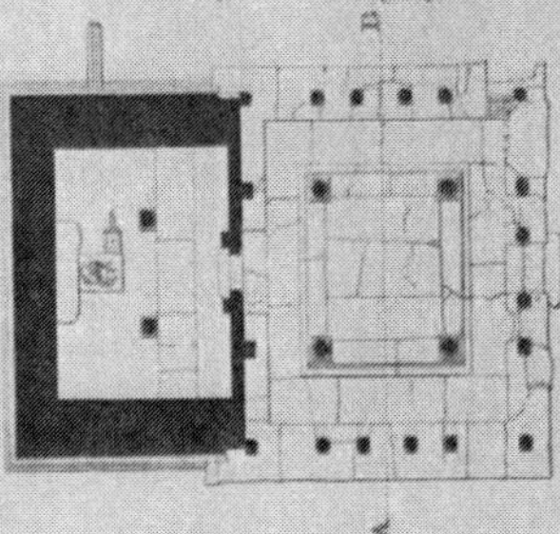

Fig. 1. Side elevation.

Fig. 3. Section A. B.

Fig. 4. Kallesvara Temple. Longitudinal Section.

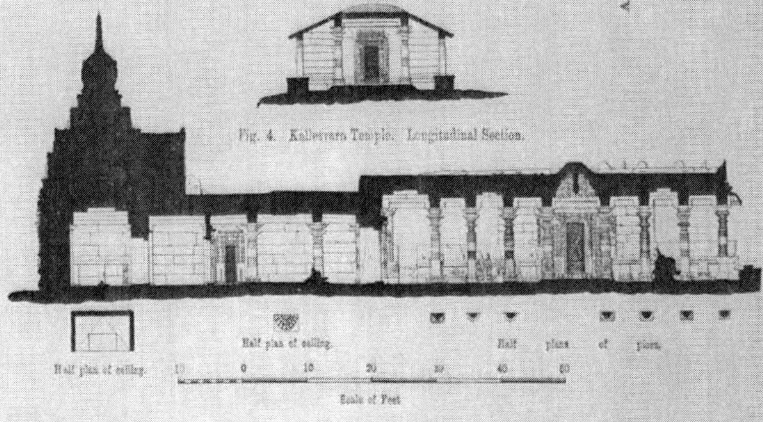

Photo-print, Survey Office, Madras.
1896.

Plate IV

BAGALI. KALLESVARA TEMPLE.

Piers in the Mahamandapa.

Photo-print, Survey Office, Madras.

PLATE V

BAGALI. KALLESVARA TEMPLE.

Fig. 1. East doorway to ardha mandapa.

Plan on line A. B.

Fig. 2. Doorway to antarala mandapa.

Plan on line C. D.

Photo-print, Survey Office, Madras.
1896

BAGALI. KALLESVARA TEMPLE.

Fig. 3. Sketch of madapalle.

Fig. 1. Elevation of south-west corner of shrine wall.

Fig. 2. Images on north wall of shrine.

12 0 1 2 3 4 5 6 7 8 9 Feet

Scale for Fig. 1.

Photo-print, Survey Office, Madras.

BAGALI KALLESVARA TEMPLE

Images in the Mahamandapa

Fig. 1. Devendra

Plate VIII

BAGALI. KALLESVARA TEMPLE.

Ceiling in the Mahamandapa.

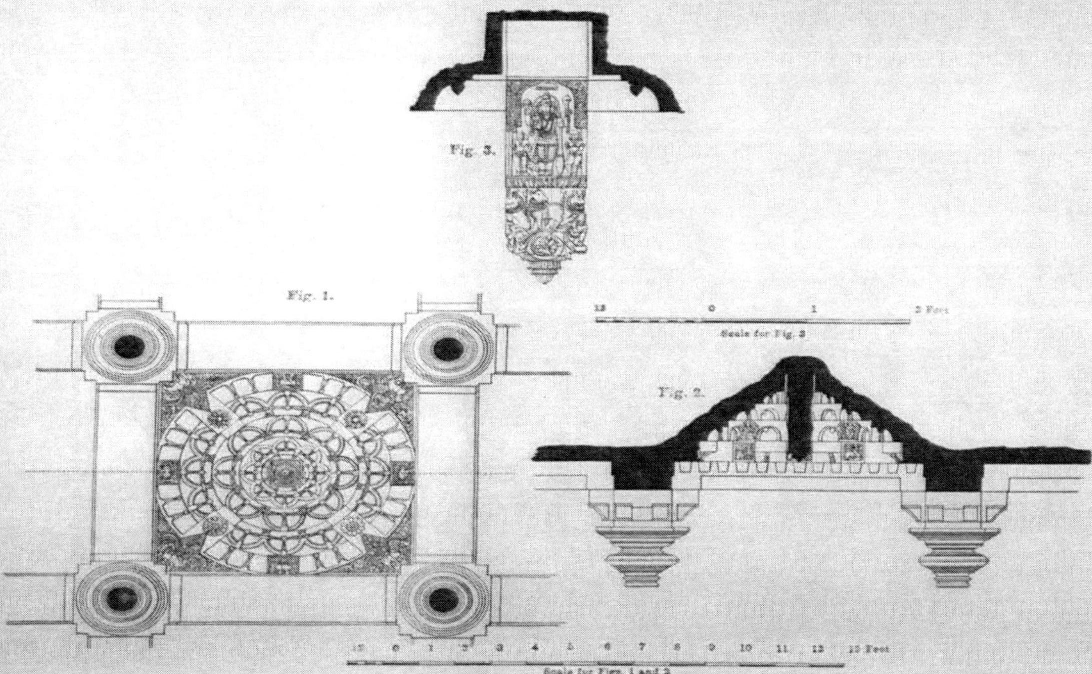

Photo-print, Survey Office, Madras.
1896

PLATE IX

MAGALA. VENUGOPALASVAMI TEMPLE.

Ground plan (ceilings dotted).

Scale of Feet

Photo-print, Survey Office, Madras.
[illegible]

MAGALA. VENUGOPALASVAMI TEMPLE.

Longitudinal Section.

Scale of feet

Photo-print Survey Office, Madras.
1899.

MAGALA. VENUGOPALASVAMI TEMPLE.

Transverse Section.

Photoprint, Survey Office, Madras.

PLATE XII

MAGALA: VENUGOPALASVAMI TEMPLE: FRONT ELEVATION.

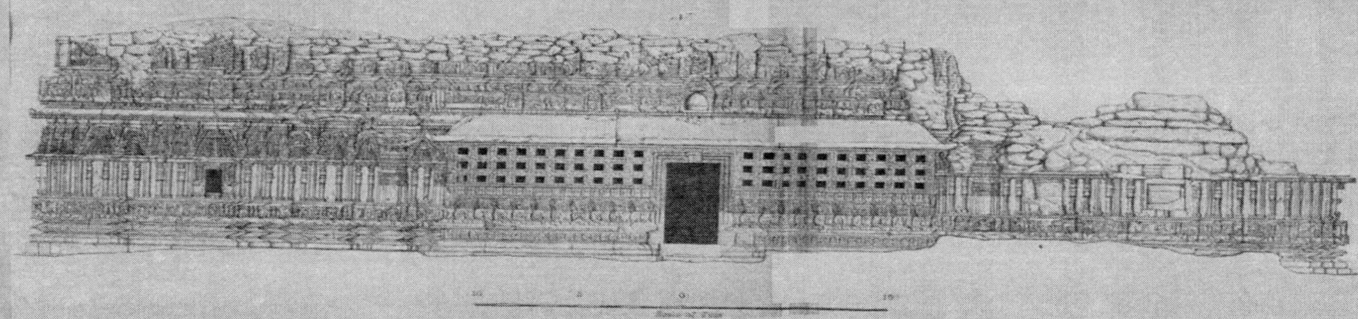

MAGALA. VENUGOPALASVAMI TEMPLE.

West Elevation.

Scale of Feet.

Photo-print, Survey Office, Madras.

PLATE XIV

MAGALA. VENUGOPALASVAMI TEMPLE.

A bay of the north wall.

Photo-print, Survey Office, Madras

PLATE XV

MADALA, VENUGOPALASVAMI TEMPLE.

Fig. 1. Ornament on base.

Fig. 2. Arched ornament over a niche.

0 3 6 9 12 Inches

Scale for Figs. 1 and 2.

HOLALU

Fig. 3. Image in a temple.

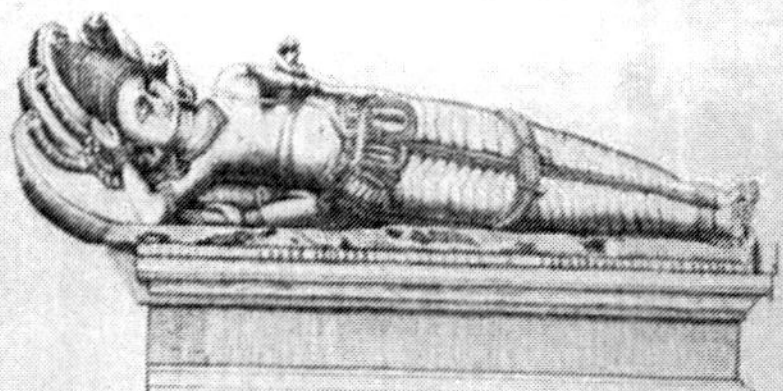

12 0 1 2 3 4 5 6 7 8 9 10 11 Feet

Scale for Fig. 3

Photozincog., Survey Office, Madras.

PLATE XVI

MAGALA. VENUGOPALASVAMI TEMPLE.

Pilaster on north side.

Scale of Feet

Photo-print, Survey Office, Madras
[illegible]

MAGALA. VENUGOPALASVAMI TEMPLE.

CENTRAL CEILING.

Plan through A. B.

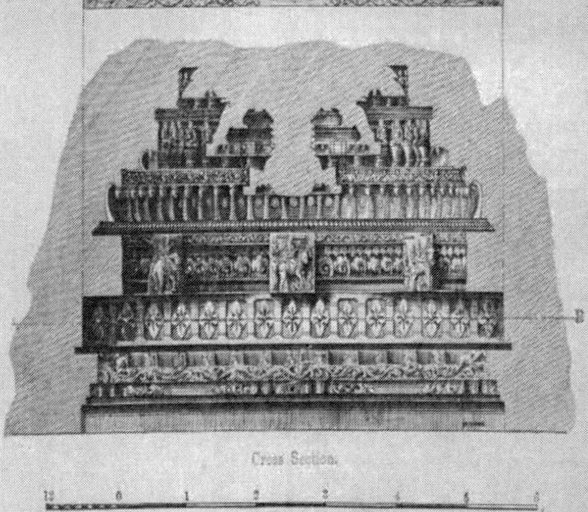

Cross Section.

12 6 1 2 3 4 5 6

Scale of Feet

Photo-print, Survey Office, Madras.
1898

PLATE XVIII

MAGALA. VENUGOPALASVAMI TEMPLE.

CEILING IN EAST END OF PORCH.

Fig. 1. Plan on A. B.

Fig. 2. Section.

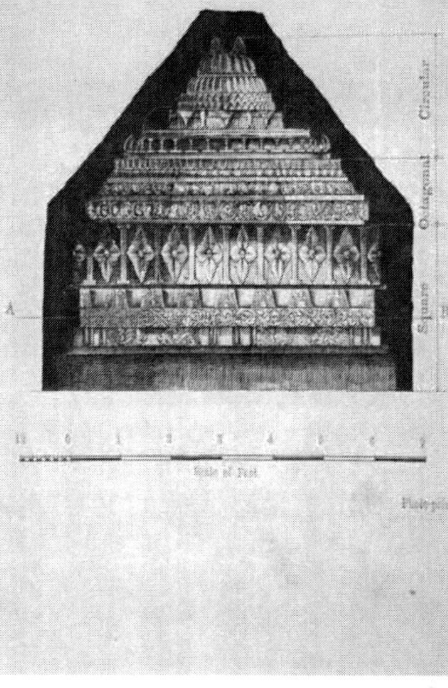

Photozinco., Survey Office, Madras
[illegible]

PLATE XIX.

MAGALA. VENUGOPALASVAMI TEMPLE.

A CEILING IN MAHAMANDAPA.

Fig. 1. Section.

Fig. 2. Plan.

Scale of Feet

Photoprint, Survey Office, Madras,

PLATE XX

…ALA. VENUGOPALASVAMI TEMPLE.

… ceiling.

Fig. 1. Plan.

Fig. 2. Section.

Inches 12 0 1 2 3 4 5 Feet

Scale of Feet

Photo-print, Survey Office, Madras

MAGALA. VENUGOPALASVAMI TEMPLE.

Cornices on niches of Mahamandapa.

Fig. 1.

Fig. 2.

Fig. 3. Panel on top of an inscribed stone.

Fig. 4. Ornament around perforated front windows.

Inches 12 6 0 1 Foot

Scale of Feet

Photoprint, Survey Office, Madras
1896

PLATE XXII

MAGALA. VENUGOPALASVAMI TEMPLE.

Image in shrine.

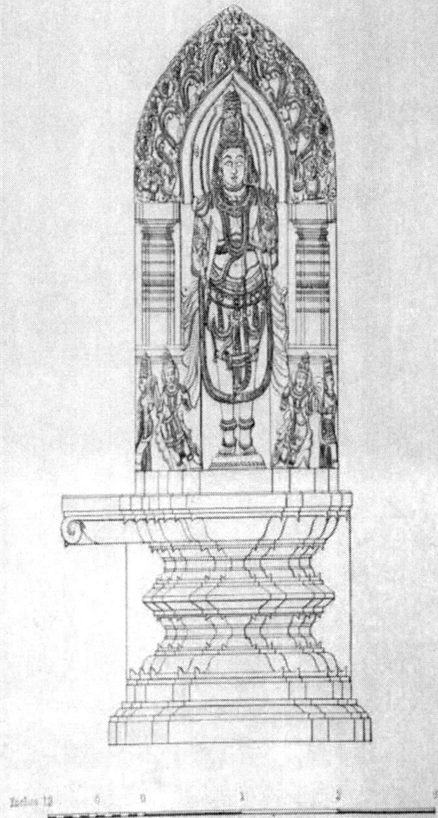

Photo-print, Survey Office, Madras.

NAGALA: VENUGOPALASVAMI TEMPLE.

Fig. 1. Somasutra.

Inches 12 6 0 1 Foot

Scale for Fig. 1

Fig. 2. Ornament on front of porch.

0 1 2 3 4 5 Inches

Scale for Fig. 2

Photo-print, Survey Office, Madras.
1896

PLATE XXIV

NAGALA: VENUGOPALASVAMI TEMPLE.

Ornaments on south side of west shrine.

Fig. 1.

Fig. 2.

Inches 12 6 0 1 Foot

Scale of Feet

Photo-print, Survey Office, Madras,
[illegible]

PLATE XXV

MAGALA. VENUGOPALASVAMI TEMPLE.

Fig. 1. Ornament over cornice.

Inches 12 6 0 1 Foot

Scale for Fig. 1

Fig. 2. Pediment over door.

0 6 12 Inches

Scale for Fig. 2

Fig. 3. On north shrine door.

0 6 Inches

Scale for Fig. 3

Photo-print, Survey Office, Madras

Plate XXVI

MAGALA. VENUGOPALASVAMI TEMPLE.

A niche on side of porch.

Inches 12 6 0 1 2 Feet

Scale of Feet

Photo-print, Survey Office, Madras

Plate XXVII

MAGALA. VENUGOPALASVAMI TEMPLE.

Architrave of a door in Mahamandapa.

Inches 12 6 0 1 Foot

Scale of Feet

Photoprint, Survey Office, Madras
[illegible]

Plate XXVIII

MAGALA. VENUGOPALASVAMI TEMPLE.

Sculptured pediment over doorway.

Photo-print, Survey Office, Madras

Plate XXIX

NAGALA. VENUGOPALASVAMI TEMPLE.

Panel with figures.

Photo-print, Survey Office, Madras.

PLATE XXX

MAGALA. VENUGOPALASVAMI TEMPLE.

Fig. 1. Pier in Mahamandapa.

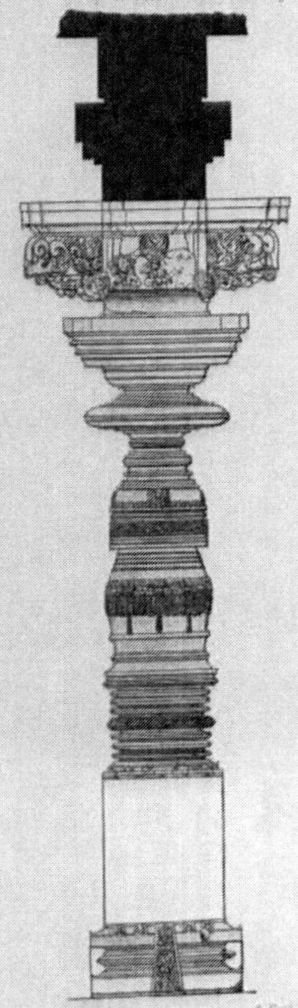

Scale for Fig. 1

Fig. 2. Sketch of pier brackets.
(no scale).

Fig. 3. Drop ornament on front cornice.

Scale for Fig. 3

Photoprint, Survey Office, Madras.

MADALA. VENUGOPALASVAMI TEMPLE.

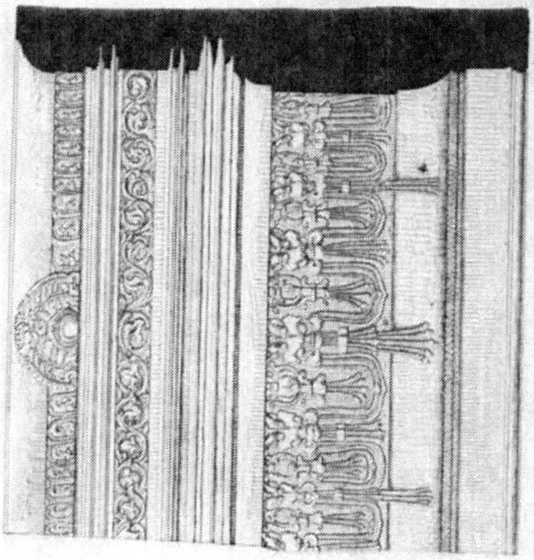

Section of pier mouldings.

Section of pier mouldings.

Photoprint, Survey Office, Madras.

PLATE XXXII

HIRAHADAGALLI KATTESVARA TEMPLE.

Plan.

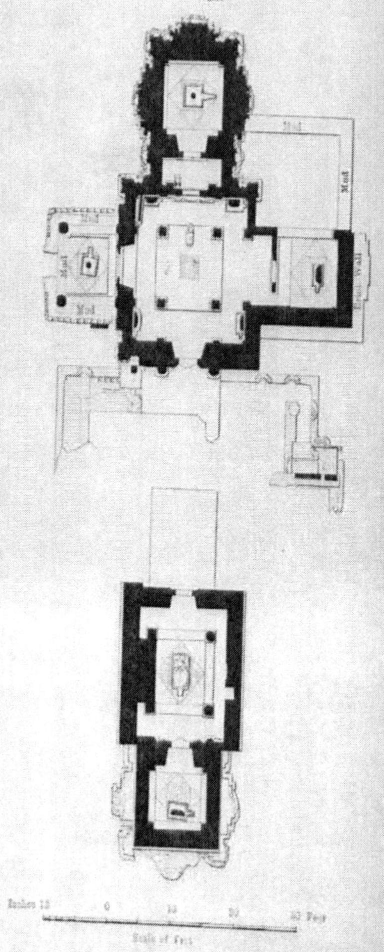

PLATE XXXIII

HIRAHADAGALLI. KATTESVARA TEMPLE.

A bay of the north wall.

Photo-print, Survey Office, Madras.

HIRAHADAGALLI. KATTESVARA TEMPLE.

Fig. 2. Central slab of a ceiling.
(Found in the ground).

Scale for Fig. 2.

Fig. 1. Bracket niche on north side.

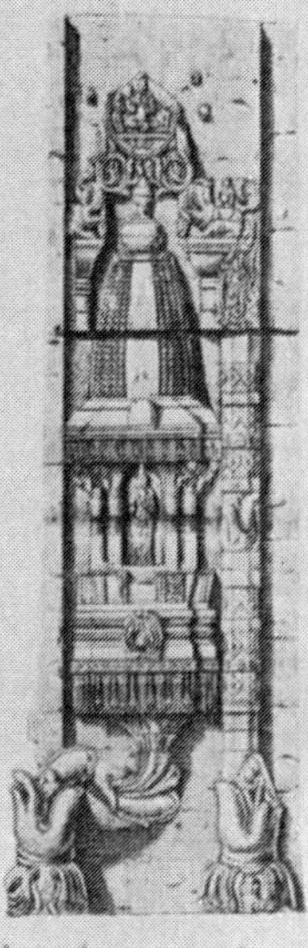

Scale for Fig. 1

Fig. 3. Panel on front cornice.

Fig. 4. Cornice block.

Scale for Fig. 3 and 4.

Photo-print, Survey Office, Madras.
[illegible]

PLATE XXXV

HIRAHADAGALLI, KATTESVARA TEMPLE: EAST DOORWAY.

Inches 12 6 0 1 2 3 4 5 6 7 Feet

Scale of Feet

Photo-print, Survey Office, Madras,
1885

PLATE XXXVI

HIRAHADAGALLI, KATTESVARA TEMPLE.

Doorway to west shrine.

Inches 12 0 3 6 9 Feet.

Scale of Feet.

Photo-print, Survey Office, Madras,
[illegible]

HIRAHADAGALLI, KATTESVARA TEMPLE.

Details of west door.

Fig. 1. Scroll ornament.

Fig. 2. Bars on perforated window.

Scale of Inches

Photo-print, Survey Office, Madras.
[illegible]

PLATE XXXVIII

HIRAHADAGALLI. KATTESVARA TEMPLE.

Fig 1. Wall ornament.

0 2 4 6 8 10 12 Inches

Scale for Fig. 1.

Fig. 2. Ornament on west wall.

0 2 4 6 8 10 12 Inches

Scale for Fig. 2

Fig. 4. Panel on wall.

0 2 4 6 Inches

Scale for Figs. 3 and 4

Fig. 3. Ornament on west door.

Photo-print, Survey Office, Madras.
1896

Plate XXXIX

HIRAHADAGALLI. KATTESVARA TEMPLE.

Fig. 1. Narayana in north shrine.

Fig. 3 Band on a pilaster on south side.

0 1 2 3 Inches

Scale for Fig. 3

Fig. 4. Drop ornament on front cornice.

0 2 4 6 Inches

Scale for Fig. 4

Fig. 2. Siva and Parvati in Mahamandapa.

Fig. 5. Band on a pilaster on south side.

0 1 2 3 Inches

Scale for Fig. 5

Inches 12 6 0 1 2 3 4 5 6 Feet

Scale for Figs. 1 and 2

Photo-print, Survey Office, Madras.
[illegible]

PLATE XL.

HIRAHADAGALLI. KATTESVARA TEMPLE.

Fig. 1. Mahishasuramardini.

Fig. 2. Sarasvati.

Fig. 3. Narayanadeva.

Inches 12 6 0 1 2 Feet

Scale for Fig. 1

Inches 12 6 0 1 2 3 4 Feet

Scale for Figs. 2 and 3

Photoprint, Survey Office, Madras,
1896

HIRAHADAGALLI. KATTESVARA TEMPLE.

Fig. 1. Cornice.

0 2 4 6 Inches

Scale for Figs. 1 and 2

Fig. 2. Cornice ornament.

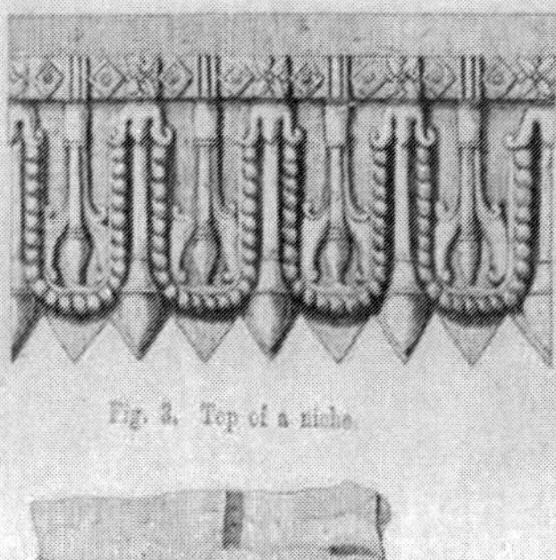

Fig. 3. Top of a niche.

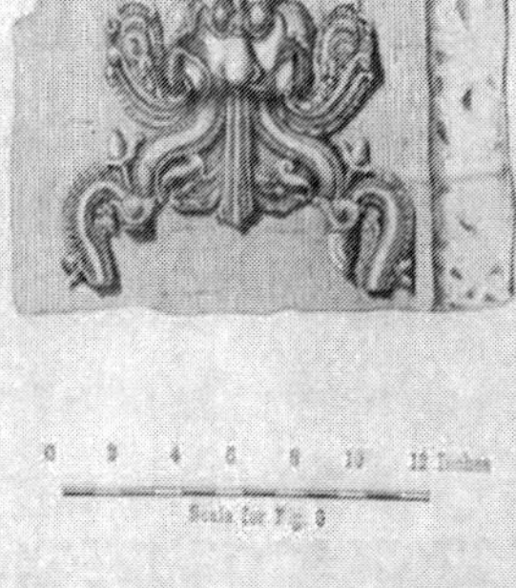

0 2 4 6 8 10 12 Inches

Scale for Fig. 3

Photo-print, Survey Office, Madras.
[illegible]

HIRAHADAGALLI, KATTESVARA TEMPLE.

Fig. 2. Base ornament.

Fig. 1. Cornice ornament.

Fig. 3. Miniature tower on south wall.

Inches 12 6 0 1 Foot

Scale for Figs. 1 and 2

Inches 12 6 0 1 Foot

Scale for Fig. 3

Photo-print, Survey Office, Madras.
[illegible]

HIRAHADAGALLI. KALLESVARA TEMPLE.

Fig. 1. Ornament on tower.

Inches 12 6 0 1 Foot

Scale of Feet

Fig. 2. Small balcony on wall.

Inches 12 6 0 1 Foot

Scale of Feet

Photo-print, Survey Office, Madras.
1896

HIRAHADAGALLI, KATTESVARA TEMPLE.

Fig. 1. Cornice ornament on tower.

Fig. 2. Top of a niche on west wall.

Inches 12 6 0 1 Foot

Scale for Fig. 1

Inches 12 6 0 1 Foot

Scale for Fig. 2

Photo-print, Survey Office, Madras.
1896

HIRAHADAGALLI. KATTESVARA TEMPLE.

Ornaments on tower.

Fig. 1.

Fig. 2.

Inches 12 6 0 1 2 Feet

Scale of Feet

Photo-print, Survey Office, Madras.
188[illegible]

HIRAHADAGALLI. KATTESVARA TEMPLE.

Fig. 1. Panel over south door.

Fig. 2. Panel over south door.

Fig. 4. Nagakal in east shrine.

Fig. 3. Pilaster capitals on north wall.

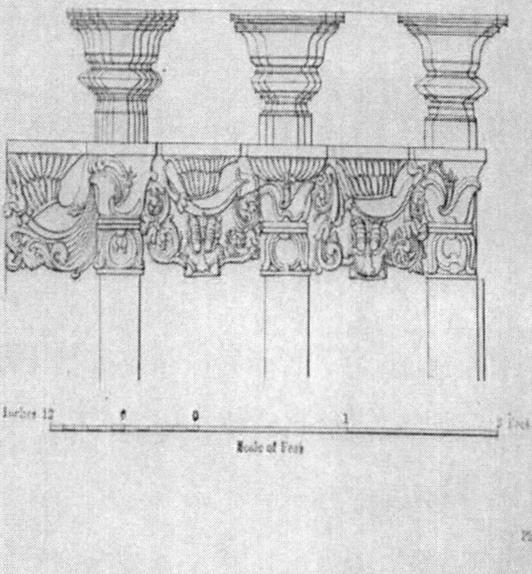

Photo-print, Survey Office, Madras.
1896

HIRAHADAGALLI. KATTESVARA TEMPLE.

Fig. 1. Pier in south porch.

Fig. 2. Pier in east temple.

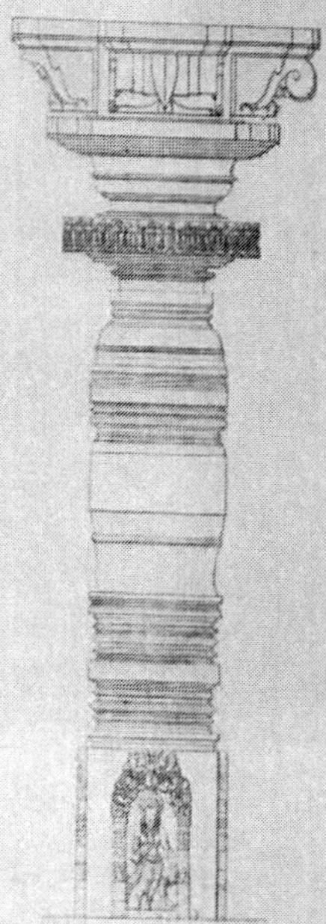

Inches 12 6 3 1 2 Feet

Scale of Feet

Photo-print, Survey Office, Madras.

NILAGUNDA. BHIMESVARA TEMPLE.

Plan.

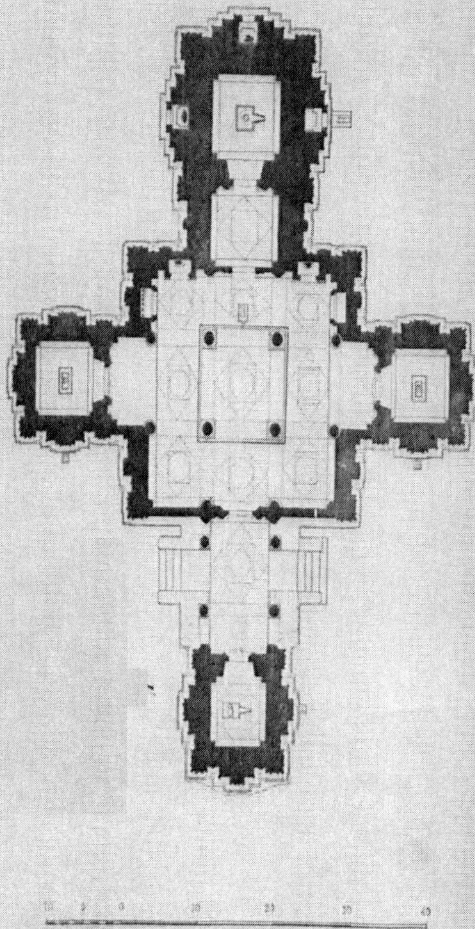

Photo-print, Survey Office, Madras.
[illegible]

PLATE XLIX

NILAGUNDA. BHIMESVARA TEMPLE.

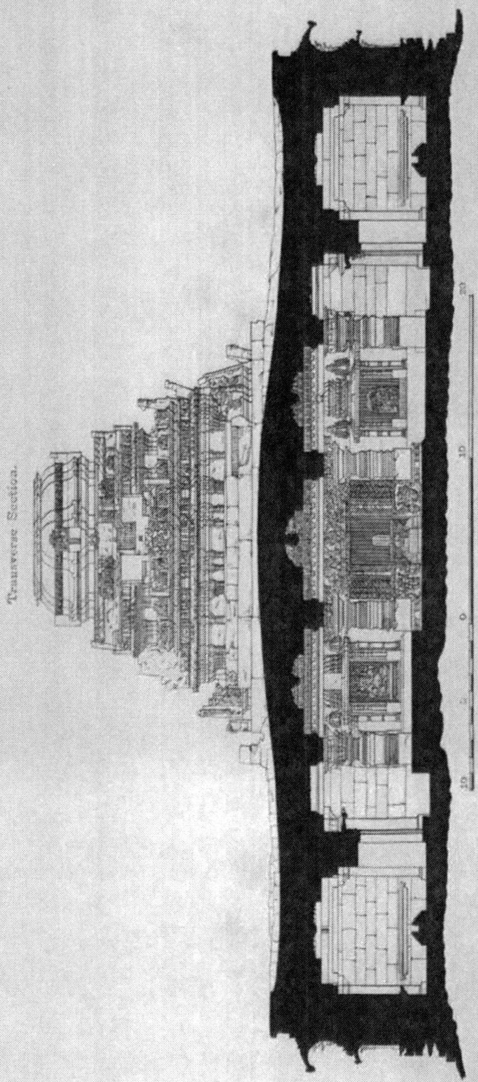

Photo-print, Survey Office, Madras.
[illegible]

Plate L.

NILAGUNDA. BHIMESVARA TEMPLE.

Side Elevation.

Scale of Feet

Photoprint, Survey Office, Madras.

NILAGUNDA. BHIMESVARA TEMPLE.

Fig. 2. Sculpture on shrine base.

Plan.

0 3 6 9 12 Inches

Scale for Fig. 2

Fig. 1. Pier in the Mahamandapa.

Plan of pier.

Inches 12 0 1 2 3 Feet

Scale for Fig. 1

Fig. 3

Tower ornaments.

Fig. 4

Inches 12 6 0 1 2 Feet

Scale for Figs. 3 and 4

Photo-print, Survey Office, Madras.
[illegible]

NILAGUNDA. BHIMESVARA TEMPLE.

Fig. 3. Plan of central ceiling.

Fig. 1. Dvarapalakas at the shrine door.

Inches 12 6 6 1 Foot

Scale for Fig. 1

Fig. 2. Dvarapalakas at the shrine door.

Fig. 4. Section of central ceiling.

0 1 2 3 4 5 6 7 8 Feet

Scale for Figs. 3 and 4

Inches 12 6 6 1 2 Feet

Scale for Fig. 2

Photoprint, Survey Office, Madras.
[illegible]

PLATE LIII

NILAGUNDA. SCULPTURES FROM VARIOUS TEMPLES.

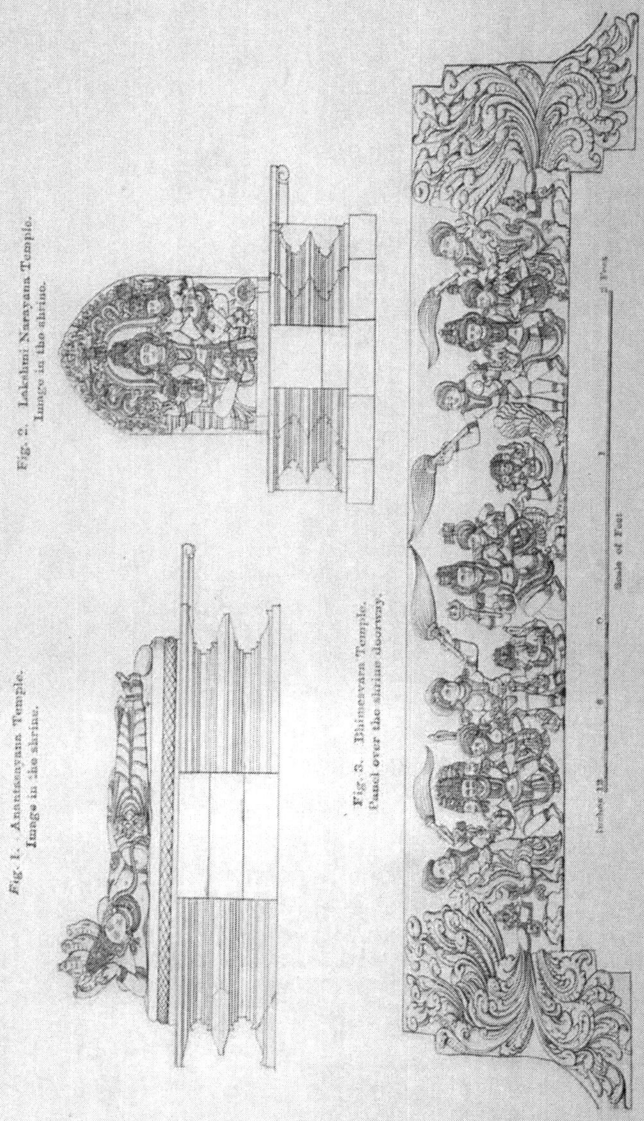

Fig. 1. Anantasayana Temple. Image in the shrine.

Fig. 2. Lakshmi Narayana Temple. Image in the shrine.

Fig. 3. Bhimesvara Temple. Panel over the shrine doorway.

Photo-print, Survey Office, Madras.
1896

Plate LIV

NILAGUNDA. BHIMESVARA TEMPLE.

Door to central shrine.

Plan.

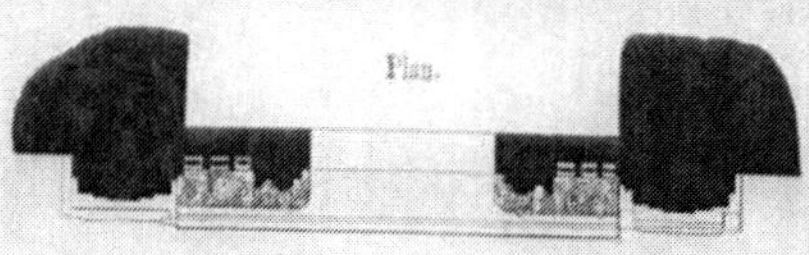

Inches 12 0 1 2 3 4 5 Feet
Scale of Feet

Photo-print, Survey Office, Madras.
[illegible]

NILAGUNDA. BHIMESVARA TEMPLE.

Somasutra on east side of shrine.

Fig. 1. Side.

Fig. 2. Front.

Fig. 3. Angle ornament on cornice.

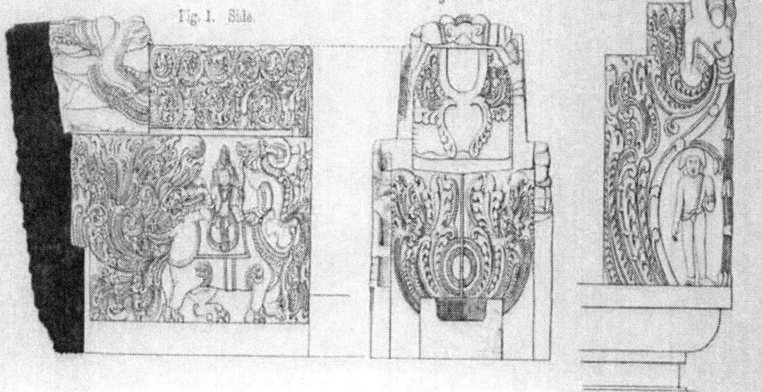

Inches 12 6 0 1 2 3 Feet

Scale of Feet

Photo-print, Survey Office, Madras.

PLATE LVI

KURUVATTI. MALIKARJUNA TEMPLE.

Plan.

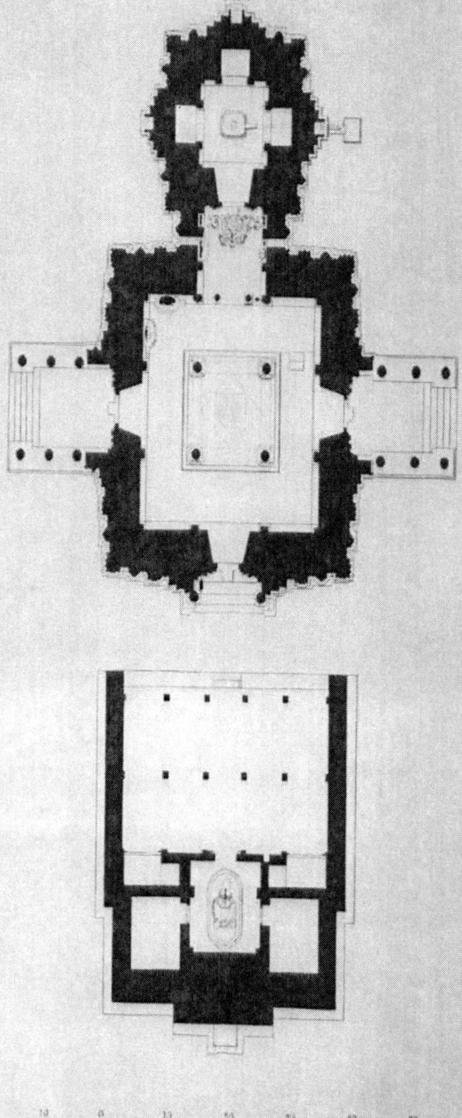

Scale of Feet

KURUVATTI. MALLIKARJUNA TEMPLE. Plate LVII

Front Elevation.

Scale of Feet.

Photo-print, Survey Office, Madras.

Plate LVIII

KURUVATTI. MALLIKARJUNA TEMPLE.

Side elevation.

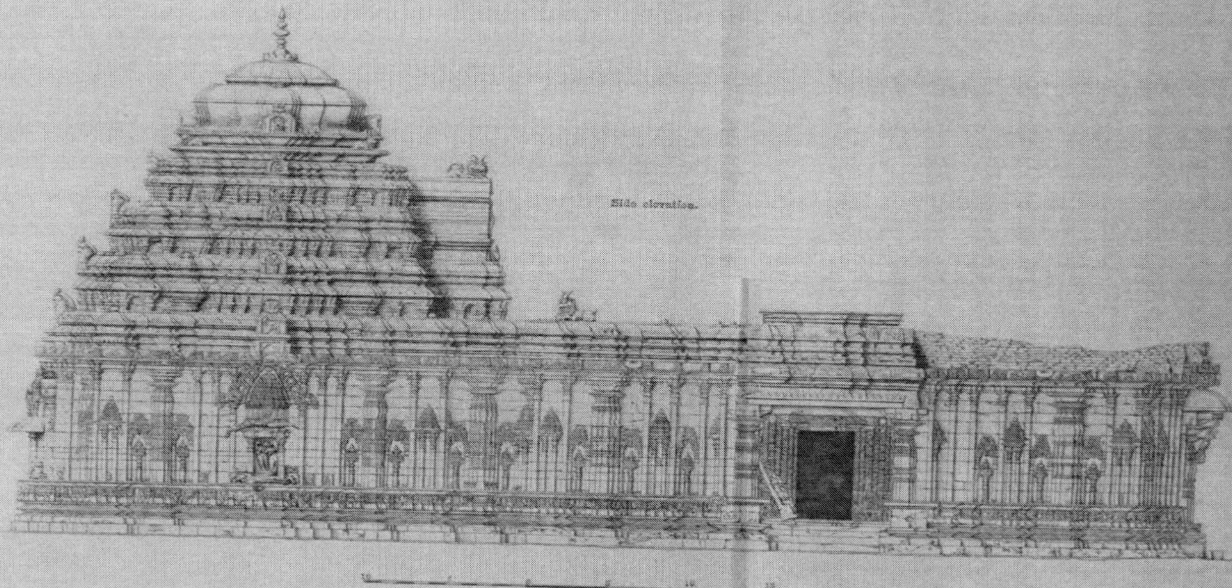

Scale of Feet

Photoprint, Survey Office, Madras.

KURUVATTI. MALIKARJUNA TEMPLE.

Fig. 1. Pier in Mahamandapa.

Fig. 2. Niche in wall.

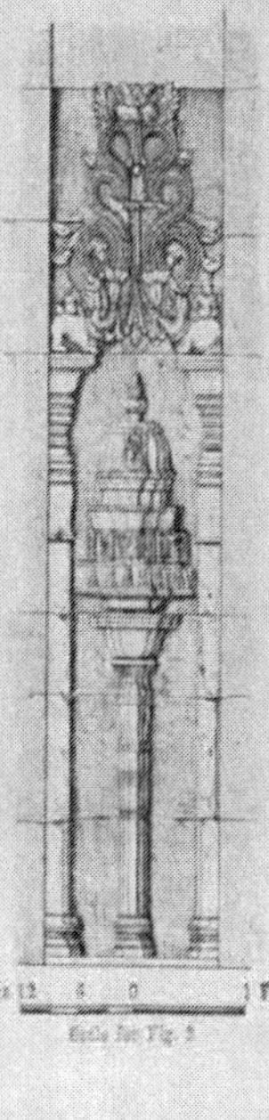

Inches 12 6 0 1 Foot

Scale for Fig. 2

Fig. 3. Pier at side of south door.

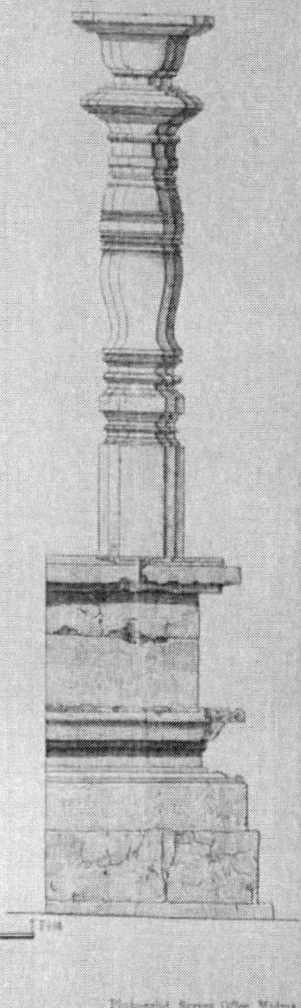

Inches 12 6 0 1 2 3 4 5 6 7 Feet

Scale for Figs. 1 and 3

Photo-print, Survey Office, Madras.

KURUVATTI. MALIKARJUNA TEMPLE. EAST ENTRANCE DOORWAY.

Photo-print, Survey Office, Madras.
1896

PLATE LXI

KURUVATTI. MALIKARJUNA TEMPLE.

A bay of the north wall.

Inches 12 6 0 3 6 9 Feet

Scale of Feet

Photo-print, Survey Office, Madras.
1894.

Fig. 1. Toran in the Mahamandapa.

Scale for Fig. 1

Fig. 3. Carved wooden door in the front mandapa.

Scale for Fig. 3

Fig. 2. Panel over south door.

Scale for Fig. 2

Fig. 4. Ornament on the east door.

Fig. 5. Foliage on the south door.

Scale for Figs. 4 and 5

KURUVATTI. MALIKARJUNA TEMPLE.

ARCHITRAVE ORNAMENTS.

Fig. 1. On north door.

Fig. 2. On north door.

Fig. 3. On east door.

Fig. 4. On east door.

Fig. 5. Mantram on a stone at Kattibinuru.

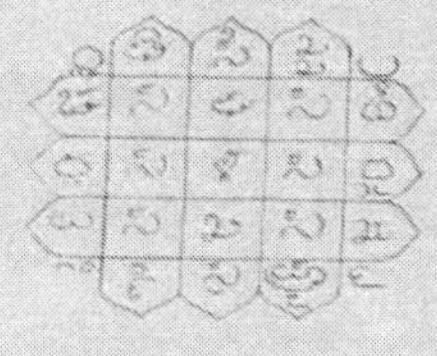

Inches 12 6 0 7 Feet

Scale of Feet

Photo-print, Survey Office, Madras.
1886

KURUVATTI. MALIKARJUNA TEMPLE.

Fig. 1. Brass mask for linga.

Fig. 2. Brass image of Siva.

Inches 12 6 0 1 2 Feet

Scale of Feet

Photoprint, Survey Office, Madras.

KURUVATTI. MALIKARJUNA TEMPLE.

Fig. 1. Brass mask for linga.

Inches 12 6 0 1 Foot

Scale for Fig. 1

Fig. 3. Ornament over a niche.

Inches 12 6 0 1 Foot

Scale for Fig. 3

Fig. 2. Sculptured stone in the road.

Inches 12 6 0 1 2 3 Feet

Scale for Fig. 2

Fig. 4 Ornament on door architrave.

0 3 6 Inches

Scale for Fig. 4

Photo-print, Survey Office, Madras.
[illegible]

PLATE LXVI

KURUVATTI. MALIKARJUNA TEMPLE.

Fig. 1. Sculptured slab at south door.

Fig. 2. Narayana.

Inches 12 6 0 1 2 3 4 Feet

Scale of Feet

Photo-print, Survey Office, Madras,
[illegible]

KURUVATTI. MALIKARJUNA TEMPLE.

Silver ornaments.

Fig. 1.

Fig. 4. Silver waist belt.

Fig. 2.

Fig. 3.

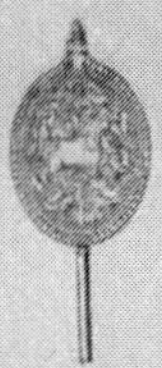

0 3 6 Inches.

Scale for Figs. 1 to 3

Fig. 5. Star step block (lying in road)

Inches 12 6 0 1 Foot

Scale for Fig 5

Photoprint, Survey Office, Madras.

Plate LXVIII

KURUVATTI. MALIKARJUNA TEMPLE.

FACING FIGURE BRACKETS OVER CAPITALS OF EAST DOOR.

Fig. 1. At right inner face.

Fig. 2. At left inner face.

Inches 12 6 0 1 2 3 Feet

Scale of Feet

Photo-print, Survey Office, Madras.
[illegible]

HUVINAHADGALLI, KALLESVARA TEMPLE.

Plan.

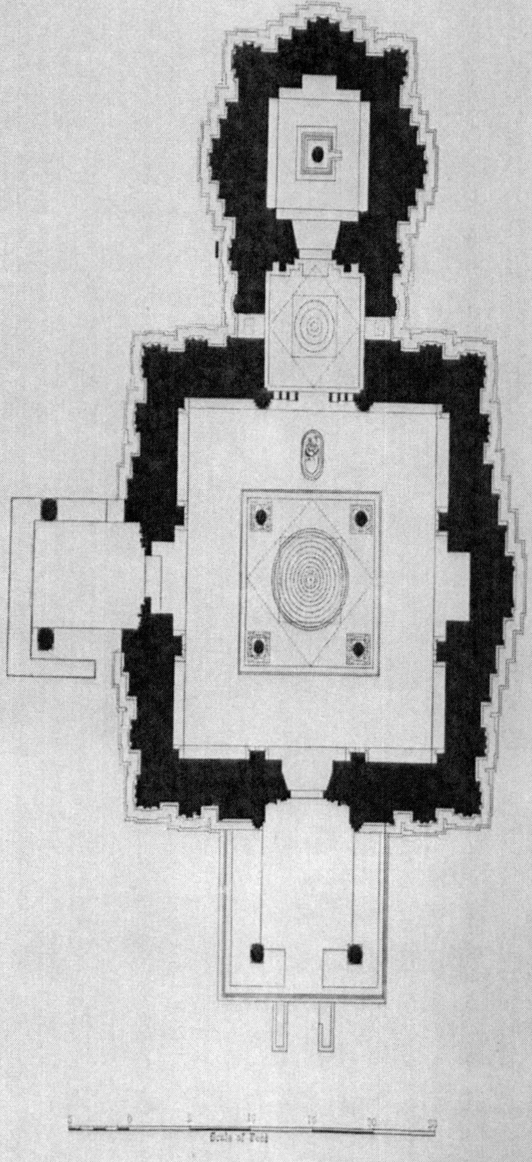

Scale of Feet

Photo-print, Survey Office, Madras.

PLATE LXX

HUVINAHADGALLI. KALLESVARA TEMPLE.

Transverse section.

Inches 12 0 1 2 3 4 5 6 7 8 9 10 11 12 13 14 15 16 17 18 19 Feet

Scale of Feet

Photo-print, Survey Office, Madras,
[illegible]

PLATE LXXI

HUVINAHADDALLI. KALLESVARA TEMPLE.

North elevation.

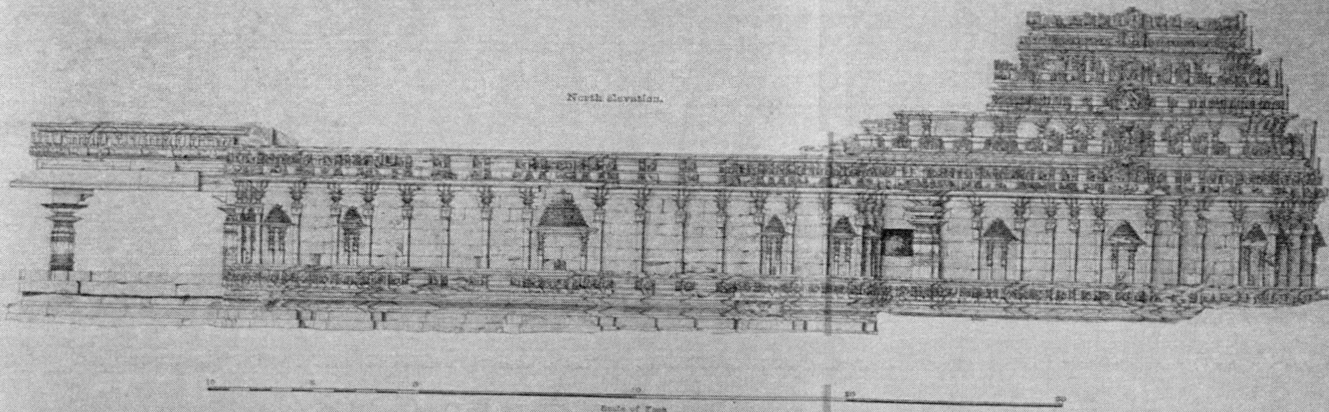

Photoprint, Survey Office, Madras.

HUVINAHADGALLI. KALLESVARA TEMPLE.

Front elevation.

Inches 12 0 1 2 3 4 5 6 7 8 9

Scale of Feet

Photo-print, Survey Office, Madras.
[illegible]

PLATE LXXIII

HUVINAHADGALLI. KALLESVARA TEMPLE.

Back elevation.

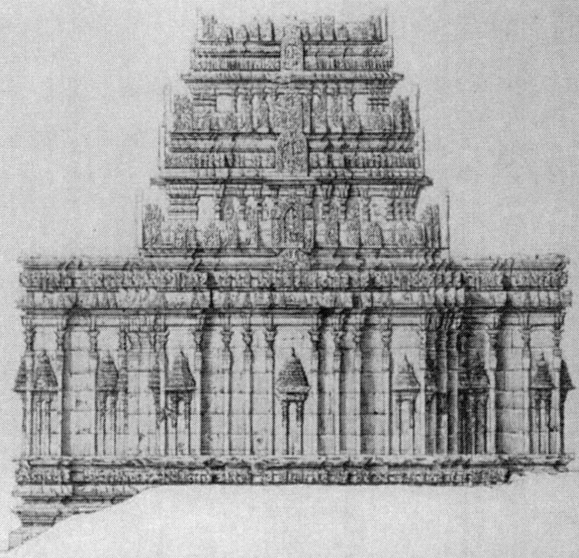

Inches 12 0 1 2 3 4 5 6 7 8 9 10 11 12 13 14 15 Feet

Scale of Feet

Photo-print, Survey Office, Madras.
[illegible]

PLATE LXXIV

HUVINAHADGALLI. KALLESVARA TEMPLE.

South door.

Inches 12 6 0 1 2 3 4 Feet

Scale of Feet

Photo-print, Survey Office, Madras.
1896.

HUVINAHADGALLI. KALLESVARA TEMPLE.

Centre bay of back wall.

Inches 12 6 0 1 2 3 4 5 Feet

Scale of Feet

Photo-print, Survey Office, Madras,
[illegible]

Plate LXXVI

HUVINAHADGALLI. KALLESVARA TEMPLE.

Fig. 1. Pier in mandapa.

Scale for Fig. 1

Fig. 2. Details of main base.

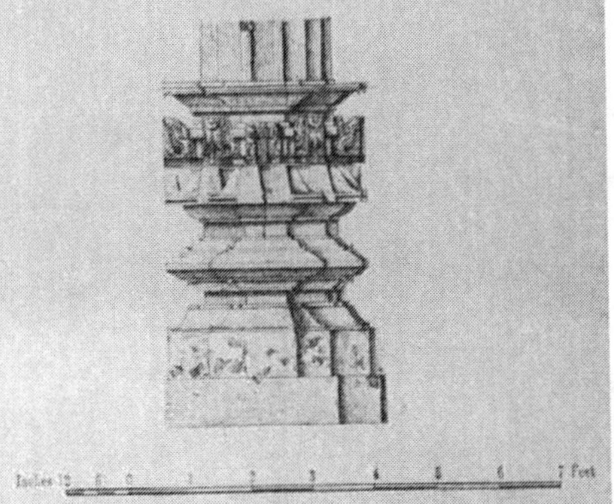

Scale for Fig. 2

Photo-print, Survey Office, Madras.
[illegible]

HUVINAHADGALLI. KALLESVARA TEMPLE.

Fig. 1. Base ornament.

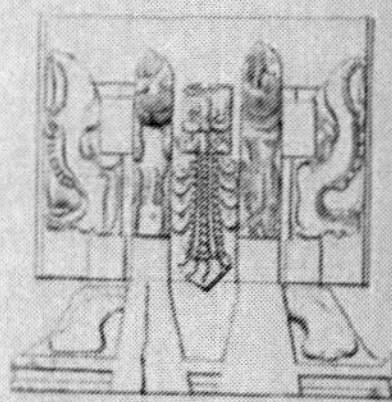

Inches 12 6 0 1 Foot

Scale for Fig. 1

Fig. 2. Ganesa.

Fig. 3. Nagakal.

Fig. 4. Balabhairava.

Fig. 5. Narayana.

Inches 12 6 0 1 2 3 4 5 6 Feet

Scale for Figs. 2 to 5

Photo-print, Survey Office, Madras.
[illegible]

HUVINAHADGALLI. KALLESVARA TEMPLE.

Fig. 1. Pilaster in Mahamandapa.

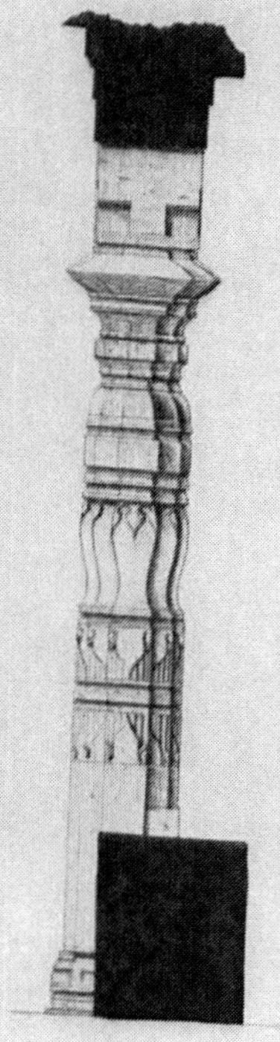

Fig. 2. Pilaster in south porch.

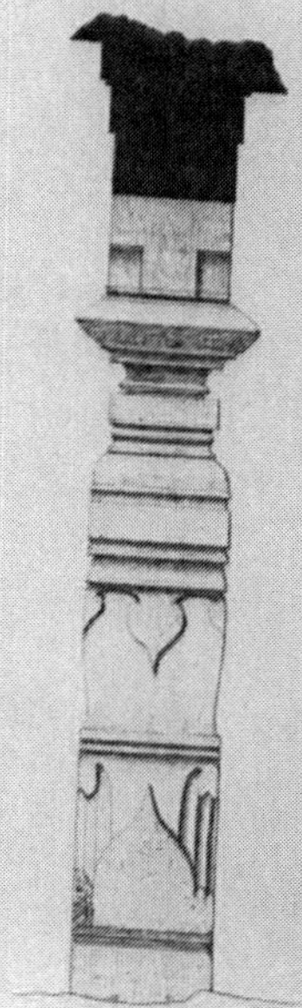

Inches 12 6 9 1 2 3 4 5 Feet

Scale of Feet

Photo-print, Survey Office, Madras.
[illegible]

PLATE LXXIX

HUVINAHADGALLI: KALLESVARA TEMPLE.

Tower cornices.

Fig. 1.

Fig. 2.

Scale of Inches

Photo-print, Survey Office, Madras.
[illegible]

PLATE LXXX

HUVINAHADGALLI. KALLESVARA TEMPLE.

Fig. 1. Ornament on tower.

Inches 12 6 0 1 2 Feet

Scale for Fig. 1

Fig. 2. Slab in road near the temple.

Inches 12 6 0 1 2 Feet

Scale for Fig. 2

Photo-print, Survey Office, Madras

HUVINAHADGALLI. KALLESVARA TEMPLE.

Cornice and sculptured block on lower.

Inches 12 6 0 1 Foot

Scale of Feet

Photo print, Survey Office, Madras.
[illegible]

PLATE LXXXII

HUVINAHADGALLI. KALLESVARA TEMPLE.

Tower ornaments.

Fig. 1.

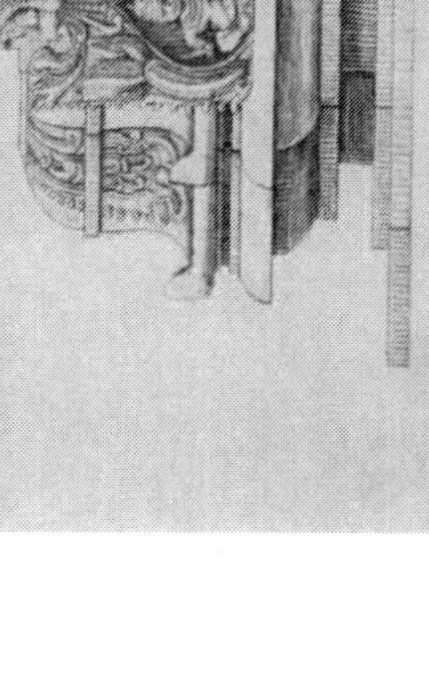

Fig. 2.

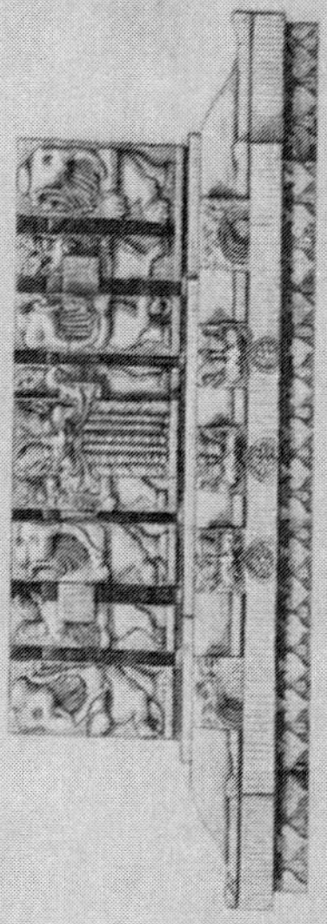

Inches 12 6 0 1 2 Feet

Scale of Feet

Photo-print, Survey Office, Madras.
[illegible]

HUVINAHADGALLI. KALLESVARA TEMPLE.

Block on tower.

Inches 12 6 0 1 Foot

Scale of Feet

Photoprint, Survey Office, Madras.
[illegible]

PLATE LXXXIV

HUVINAHADAGALLI. KALLESVARA TEMPLE.

DETAILS FROM THE TOWER.

Fig. 1.

Fig. 2.

0 2 4 6 8 10 12 14

Scale of Inches

Photo-print, Survey Office, Madras.
[illegible]

HUVINAHADGALLI. KALLESVARA TEMPLE.

Cornice blocks.

Fig. 1.

Fig. 2.

0 3 6 9 12 Inches

Scale for Fig. 2

Inches 12 6 0 1 Foot

Scale for Fig. 1

Photo-print, Survey Office, Madras.
[illegible]

HUVINAHADGALLI. KALLESVARA TEMPLE.

Angle cornice blocks.

Fig. 1.

0 3 6 9 12 Inches

Scale for Fig. 1

Fig. 2.

0 3 6 9 12 Inches

Scale for Fig. 2

Photo-print, Survey Office, Madras.
[illegible]

PLATE LXXXVII

HUVINAHADGALLI. KALLESVARA TEMPLE.

Large cornice block.

Inches 12 9 6 3 0 1 Foot

Scale of Feet

Photoprint, Survey Office, Madras.
[illegible]

PLATE LXXXVIII

HUVINAHADGALLI. KALLESVARA TEMPLE.

Portion of north side wall.

Inches 12 6 0 1 2 3 4 5 Feet

Scale of Feet

Photo-print, Survey Office, Madras.
[illegible]

HUVINAHADGALLI. KALLESVARA TEMPLE.

Fig. 2. Main cornice.

Fig. 1. Nandi in Mahamandapa.

…hes 12 6 0 1 2 3 Ft.

Scale for Fig. 1

Ins. 12 6 0 1 Foot

Scale for Fig. 2

Photo-print, Survey Office, Madras
[illegible]

PLATE XC

HUVINAHADGALLI. KALLESVARA TEMPLE.

Fig. 1. Panel over front gateway.

Fig. 2. Nagakal.

Fig. 3. Nagakal.

Inches 12 6 0 1 Foot

Scale for Fig. 1

Inches 12 6 0 1 Foot

Scale for Figs. 2 and 3

Photo-print, Survey Office, Madras.
[illegible]

HUVINAHADAGALI. KALLESVARA TEMPLE.

Details of tower.

Inches 12 6 0 1 2 Feet

Scale of Feet

Photo-print, Survey Office, Madras.
[illegible]

Plate XCII

HUVINAHADGALLI. KESAVASVAMI TEMPLE.

Plan.

Scale of Feet

Photo-print, Survey Office, Madras,
[illegible]

Plate XCIII

HUVINAHADGALLI. KESAVASVAMI TEMPLE.

Front elevation.

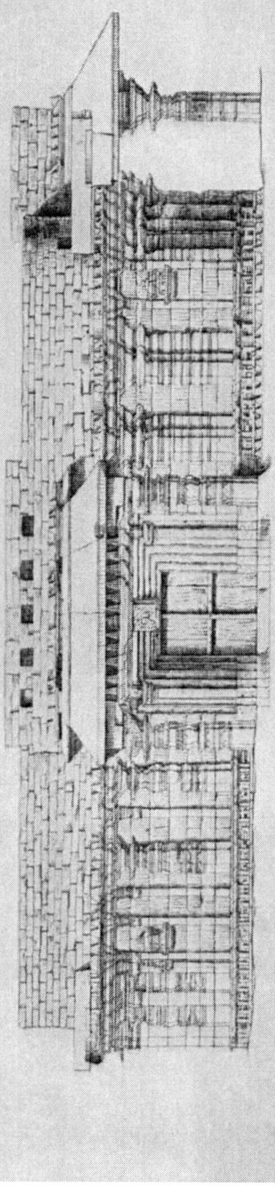

Scale of Feet

Photo-print, Survey Office, Madras.

HUVINAHADGALLI. KESAVASVAMI TEMPLE.

Side elevation.

Photoprint, Survey Office, Madras.

HUVINAHADGALLI. KRISHNASVAMI TEMPLE.

Shrine doorway.

5 4 3 2 1 0 5

Scale of Feet

Photo-print, Survey Office, Madras.
[illegible]

PLATE XCVI

HUVINAHADGALLI, KESAVASVAMI TEMPLE.

Fig. 1. Pier.

Fig. 2. Yoganarasimha.

Fig. 3. Ganesa.

Inches 12 6 0 1 2 3 4 Feet

Scale for Fig. 1

Inches 12 6 0 1 Foot

Scale for Figs. 2 and 3

Photo-print, Survey Office, Madras.
1896

HUVINAHADGALLI. KESAVASVAMI TEMPLE.

Image in shrine.

Inches 12 6 0 1 2 3 4 5 Feet

Scale of Feet

Photo-print, Survey Office, Madras
[illegible]

HUVINAHADGALLI.

Various carvings.

Fig. 1. Linga at a small temple near the tank.

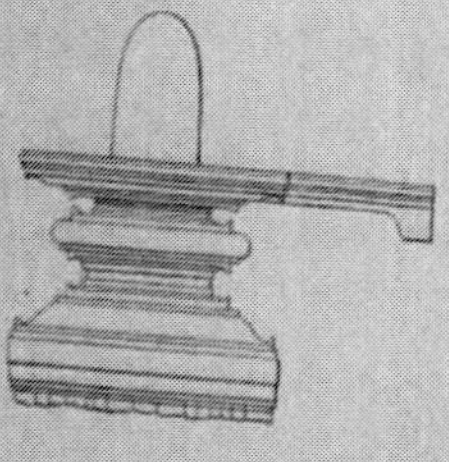

Fig. 2. Nagakal at the tank.

Inches 12 6 0 1 2 Feet

Scale for Figs. 1 to 3

Fig. 3. Nagamani and Nagakanya at the tank.

Fig. 4. Figure bracket on a pilaster at the [illegible] temple.

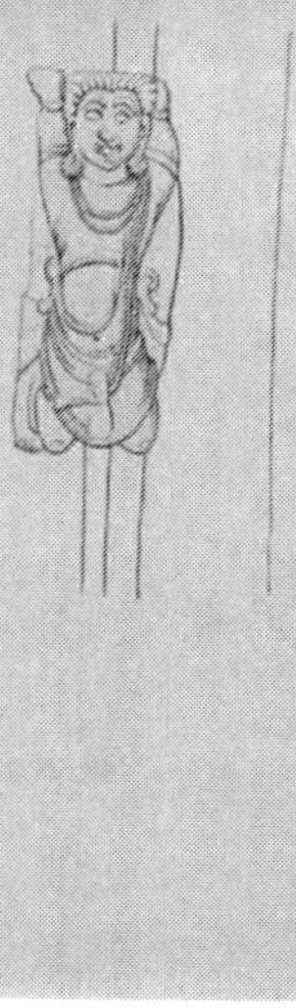

0 2 4 6 8 Inches

Scale for Fig. 4

Photoprint, Survey Office, Madras.
[illegible]

Plate C

HUVINAHADGALLI

Fig. 1. Nagakal in a field.

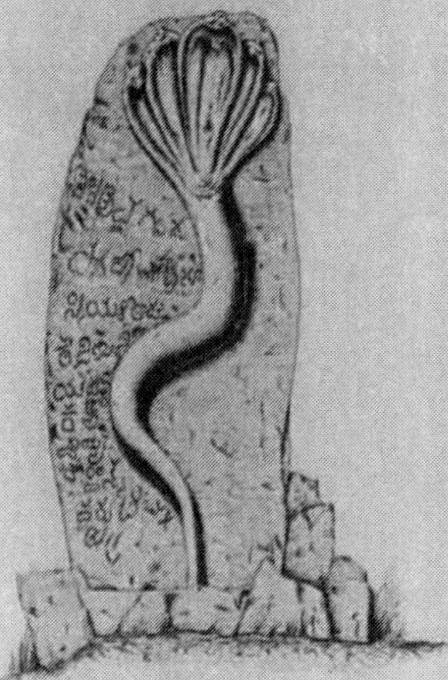

Inches 12 6 0 1 Foot

Scale for Fig. 1

Fig. 2. Ornament on piers in porch at [illegible] temple

Inches 12 6 0 1 Foot

Scale for Fig. 2

Photo-print, Survey Office, Madras.
[illegible]

PLATE CI

HUVINAHADGALLI. HANUMAN TEMPLE.

Jamb ornaments on the east door.

Fig. 1. Nagendra and Nagakanya.

Fig. 2.

Fig. 3.

0 6 12 Inches

Scale for Fig. 1

0 3 6 9 12 Inches

Scale for Figs. 2 and 3

Photo-print, Survey Office, Madras.
1896

PLATE CII

HUVINAHADGALLI. KESAVASVAMI TEMPLE.

Plan.

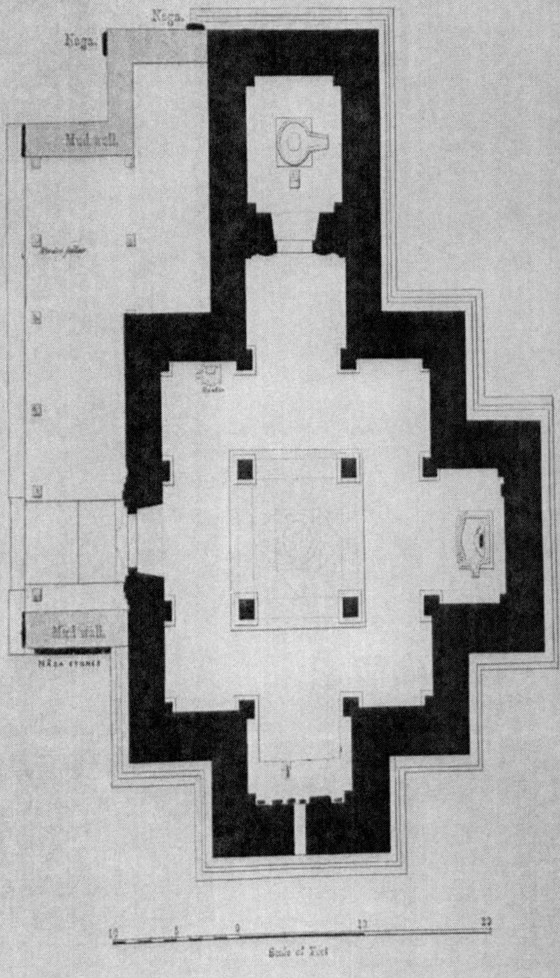

Photo-print, Survey Office, Madras.

HALAVAGALU. KALLESVARA TEMPLE.

Fig. 1. Pier in Mahamandapa.

Inches 12 6 0 1 2 3 Feet

Scale for Fig. 1

Fig. 2. Image in shrine.

Inches 12 6 0 1 Foot

Scale for Fig. 2

Photoprint, Survey Office, Madras.

PLATE CIV

HALAVAGALU. KALLESVARA TEMPLE.

Sculptured slab.

Photoprint, Survey Office, Madras

HALAVAGALU. KALLESVARA TEMPLE.

Sculptured slabs.

Fig. 1.

Fig. 2.

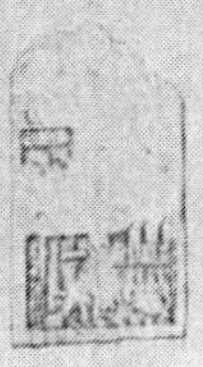

Fig. 3.

Scale for Fig. 3

Scale for Fig. 1

Scale for Fig. 2

Photoprint, Survey Office, Madras.

HARIHAR: HARIHARESVARA TEMPLE.

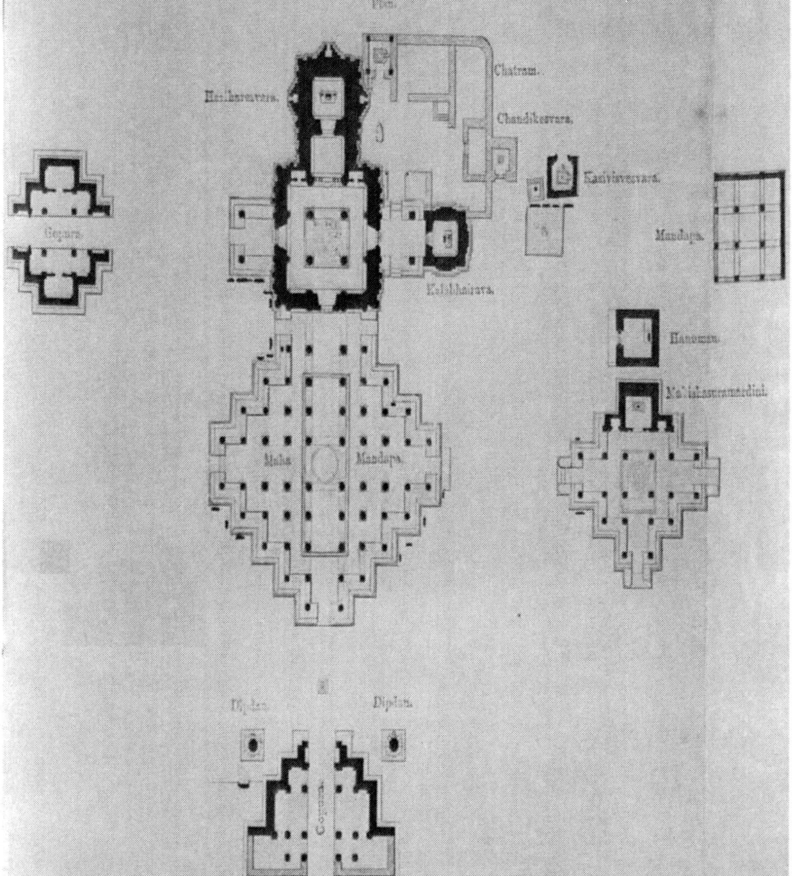

Photozinco, Survey Office, Madras.

HARIHAR. HARIHARESVARA TEMPLE.

CEILING IN THE ANTARALA MANDAPA.

Inches 12 6 0 1 2 3 4 5 10 Feet

Scale of Feet.

Photo-print, Survey Office, Madras.
1896.

PLATE CVIII

HARIHAR, HARIHAREŚVARA TEMPLE.

CEILING IN THE AMMAN TEMPLE.

Photo-print, Survey Office, Madras.
1896

PLATE CIX.

HARIHAR. HARIHARESVARA TEMPLE.

Fig. 1. Dipdan or Dipastambha.

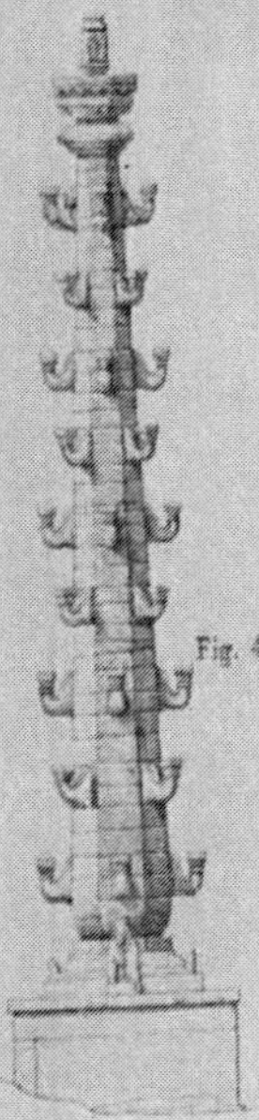

Fig. 3. Kalabhairava.

0 3 6 9 12 Inches

Scale for Fig. 3

Fig. 4. Sculptured slab.

Fig. 5. Architrave on the entrance to the Kalabhairava Temple.

Fig. 2. Plan of dipdan.

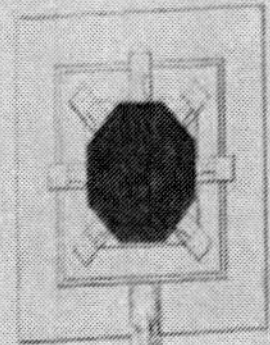

Inches 12 0 1 2 3 4 5 Ft.

Scale for Figs. 1 and 2

Inches 12 6 0 1 Foot

Scale for Fig. 4

0 3 6 9 12 Inches

Scale for Fig. 5

Photo-print, Survey Office, Madras

[illegible]

PLATE CX

HARIHAR. HARIHARESVARA TEMPLE.

CEILING IN MAHAMANDAPA.

Fig. 1. Plan.

Fig. 2. Section thro A. B.

Photo-print, Survey Office, Madras.

Plate CXI

HARIHAR. HARIHARESVARA TEMPLE.

Fig. 1. North-east corner of shrine wall.

Scale for Fig. 1

Fig. 2. Entrance to Kalabhairava Temple.

Fig. 3. Plan on line A. B.

Scale for Figs. 2 and 3

Photo-print, Survey Office, Madras.
[illegible]

PLATE CXII

HARIHAR. HARIHARESVARA TEMPLE.

Fig. 1. Image in the shrine.

Inches 12 0 1 2 3 Feet

Scale for Fig. 1.

Ornamental details of the wall base.

Fig. 2.

Fig. 3.

Fig. 4.

Inches 12 6 0 1 2 3 Feet

Scale for Figs 2 to 4

Photo-print, Survey Office, Madras.
[illegible]

PLATE CXIII

HARIHAR. HARIHARESVARA TEMPLE.

Fig. 1. Door architrave at Mahamandapa.

Fig. 2. Carved scroll on door of Mahamandapa.

Scale for Fig. 2

Fig. 3. Pier in Mahamandapa.

Fig. 4. Pier at east gopura.

Half plan at C. D.

Scale for Figs. 3 and 4

Photo-print, Survey Office, Madras
1886

SIDRAHALLI.

FORT TEMPLE.

Fig. 1. Lingam in the Court.

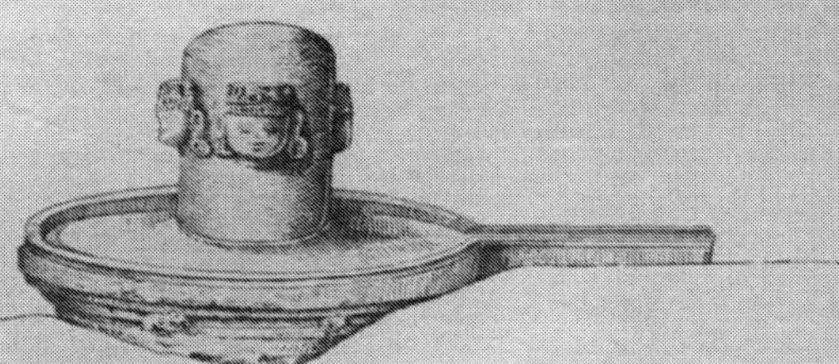

Fig. 2. Pier in Mahamandapa.

Photoprint, Survey Office, Madras.

PLATE CXIV

Published by

Facsimile Publisher
Ashok Vihar, Delhi-110052 (India)
Website: www.facsimilepublisher.com

Distributed by

Gyan Books Pvt. Ltd.
5, Ansari Road, Daryaganj, New Delhi-110002 (India)
E-mail: books@gyanbooks.com, Website: www.gyanbooks.com

2 222000 002794